EAST AND WEST

Also by Aleksandr I. Solzhenitsyn

The Oak and the Calf

The Gulag Archipelago I–II

The Gulag Archipelago III–IV

The Gulag Archipelago V–VI

Prussian Nights

Warning to the West

Lenin in Zurich

Candle in the Wind

August 1914

A Lenten Letter to Pimen, Patriarch of All Russia

Stories and Prose Poems

The Love Girl and the Innocent

Cancer Ward

The First Circle

For the Good of the Cause

We Never Make Mistakes

One Day in the Life of Ivan Denisovich

EAST AND WEST

THE NOBEL LECTURE ON LITERATURE,

A WORLD SPLIT APART,

LETTER TO THE SOVIET LEADERS,

AND AN INTERVIEW

WITH ALEKSANDR SOLZHENITSYN

BY JANIS SAPIETS

Aleksandr I. Solzhenitsyn

PERENNIAL LIBRARY

Harper & Row, Publishers

New York, Cambridge, Hagerstown, Philadelphia,
San Francisco, London, Mexico City,
São Paulo, Sydney

FIRST EDITION

Library of Congress Cataloging in Publication Data

Solzhenitsyn, Aleksandr Isaevich, 1918–
    East and West.
    (Perennial Library)
    CONTENTS: The Nobel lecture on literature.—A world split apart.—Letter to the Soviet leaders.—Interview with Aleksandr Solzhenitsyn by Janis Sapiets.
    I. Title.
PG3488. 04A245   1980   891.73′44   79–5222
ISBN 0–06–080508–0 pbk.

    80 81 82 83 10 9 8 7 6 5 4 3 2 1

CONTENTS

The Nobel Lecture on Literature (1972)   3

A World Split Apart (1978)   39

Letter to the Soviet Leaders (1973)   75

An Interview with Aleksandr Solzhenitsyn

by Janis Sapiets (1979)   145

THE NOBEL
LECTURE ON
LITERATURE

*Translated from the Russian
by Alexis Klimoff*

ONE

Just as the savage in bewilderment picks up . . . a strange object cast up by the sea? . . . something long buried in the sand? . . . a baffling object fallen from the sky?—intricately shaped, now glistening dully, now reflecting a brilliant flash of light —just as he turns it this way and that, twirls it, searches for a way to utilize it, seeks to find for it a suitable lowly application, all the while not guessing its higher function . . .

So we also, holding Art in our hands, confidently deem ourselves its masters; we boldly give it direction, bring it up to date, reform it, proclaim it, sell it for money, use it to please the powerful, divert it for amusement—all the way down to vaudeville songs and nightclub acts—or else adapt it (with a muzzle or stick, whatever is handy) toward transient political or limited social needs. But art remains undefiled by our endeavors and the stamp of its origin remains unaffected: each time and in every usage it bestows upon us a portion of its mysterious inner light.

But can we encompass the *totality* of this light? Who would dare to say that he has *defined* art? Or has enumerated all its aspects? Moreover, perhaps someone already did understand and did name them for us in the preceding centuries, but that could not long detain us: we listened briefly but took no heed; we discarded the words at once, hurrying—as always—to replace even the very best with something else, just so that it might be new. And when we are told the old once again, we won't even remember that we used to have it earlier.

One artist imagines himself the creator of an autonomous spiritual world; he hoists upon his shoulders the act of creating this world and of populating it, together with the total responsibility for it. But he collapses under the load, for no mortal genius can bear up under it, just as, in general, the man who declares himself the center of existence is unable to create a balanced spiritual system. And if a failure befalls such a man, the blame is promptly laid to the chronic disharmony of the world, to the complexity of modern man's divided soul, or to the public's lack of understanding.

Another artist recognizes above himself a higher power and joyfully works as a humble apprentice under God's heaven, though graver and more demanding still is his responsibility for all he writes or paints—and for the souls which apprehend it. However, it was not he who created this world, nor does he control it; there can be no doubts about its foundations. It is merely given to the artist to sense more keenly than others the harmony of the world, the beauty and ugliness of man's role in it—and to vividly communicate this to mankind. Even amid failure and at the lower depths of existence—in poverty, in prison, and in illness—a sense of enduring harmony cannot abandon him.

But the very irrationality of art, its dazzling convolutions, its unforeseeable discoveries, its powerful impact on men—all this is too magical to be wholly accounted for by the artist's view of the world, by his intention, or by the work of his unworthy fingers.

Archaeologists have yet to discover an early stage of human existence when we possessed no art. In the twilight preceding the dawn of mankind we received it from Hands which we did not have a chance to see clearly. Neither had we time to ask: *Why* this gift for us? How should we treat it?

All those prognosticators of the decay, degeneration, and death of art were wrong and will always be wrong. It shall be we who die; art will remain. And shall we even comprehend before our passing all of its aspects and the entirety of its purposes?

Not everything can be named. Some things draw us beyond words. Art can warm even a chilled and sunless soul to an exalted spiritual experience. Through art we occasionally receive—indistinctly, briefly—revelations the likes of which cannot be achieved by rational thought.

It is like that small mirror of legend: you look into it but instead of yourself you glimpse for a moment the Inaccessible, a realm forever beyond reach. And your soul begins to ache. . . .

TWO

Dostoyevsky once let drop an enigmatic remark: "Beauty will save the world." What is this? For a long time it seemed to me simply a phrase.

How could this be possible? When in the blood-thirsty process of history did beauty ever save any-one, and from what? Granted, it ennobled, it ele-vated—but whom did it ever save?

There is, however, a particular feature in the very essence of beauty—a characteristic trait of art itself: the persuasiveness of a true work of art is completely irrefutable; it prevails even over a resisting heart. A political speech, an aggressive piece of journalism, a program for the organiza-tion of society, a philosophical system, can all be constructed—with apparent smoothness and har-mony—on an error or on a lie. What is hidden and what is distorted will not be discerned right away. But then a contrary speech, journalistic piece, or program, or a differently structured philosophy, comes forth to join the argument, and everything is again just as smooth and harmonious, and again everything fits. And so they inspire trust—and dis-trust.

In vain does one repeat what the heart does not find sweet.

But a true work of art carries its verification within itself: artificial and forced concepts do not survive their trial by images; both image and con-cept crumble and turn out feeble, pale, and unconvincing. However, works which have drawn on the truth and which have presented it to us in concentrated and vibrant form seize us, attract us to themselves powerfully, and no one ever—even centuries later—will step forth to deny them.

So perhaps the old trinity of Truth, Goodness, and Beauty is not simply the decorous and antiquated formula it seemed to us at the time of our self-confident materialistic youth. If the tops of these three trees do converge, as thinkers used to claim, and if the all too obvious and the overly straight sprouts of Truth and Goodness have been crushed, cut down, or not permitted to grow, then perhaps the whimsical, unpredictable, and ever surprising shoots of Beauty will force their way through and soar up to *that very spot*, thereby fulfilling the task of all three.

And then no slip of the tongue but a prophecy would be contained in Dostoyevsky's words: "Beauty will save the world." For it was given to him to see many things; he had astonishing flashes of insight.

Could not then art and literature in a very real way offer succor to the modern world?

Today I shall attempt to set forth those few aspects of this problem which I have been able to discern over the years.

THREE

To have mounted this rostrum from which the Nobel Lecture is delivered—a platform placed at the disposal of but few writers and then only once in a lifetime—I have climbed not the three or four attached steps, but hundreds and even thousands of them, with almost no toehold, steep, and covered with ice, leading out of the darkness and cold where it had been my fate to survive while others —perhaps more gifted and stronger than I—perished. Only a few of them did I meet in the "Gulag Archipelago," scattered as it was into a multitude of islands. But under the burden of surveillance and mistrust I could not say much to most of them; of some I only heard; of still others I could only guess. Those who vanished into this abyss when they had already earned a literary reputation are at least known; but how many there were who had not yet been recognized, who had never been publicly named! And almost no one managed to return. An entire national literature remains there, buried without a coffin, even without underwear—naked, with only an identifying tag on one toe. Not for a moment did Russian literature cease! Yet from the outside it seemed a wasteland. Where a congenial forest might have stood there remained after all the felling but two or three trees overlooked by chance.

And today, accompanied by the shades of the fallen, as with bowed head I permit others who were worthy earlier to precede me to this platform—how am I today to surmise and to express what *they* would have wished to say?

This duty has long weighed upon us and we knew it all along. In the words of Vladimir Soloviev:

> Even in chains we must ourselves complete
> That orbit which the gods have traced for us.

In the midst of exhausting prison camp relocations, marching in a column of prisoners in the gloom of bitterly cold evenings, with strings of camp lights glimmering through the darkness, we would often feel rising in our breast what we would have wanted to shout out to the whole world—if only the whole world could have heard any one of us. It all seemed very clear then: just what our fortunate messenger would say and how the world would at once respond in turn. Our field of vision was then filled with distinct physical objects and clear psychological motivations; an unambiguous world seemed to contain nothing which could prevail against this vision. These thoughts came not from books and were not borrowed for their appearance' sake: they were forged in prison cells and around bonfires in the forest, in conversation with people now dead; they were tested by *that* life and it is *from there* that they arose.

But when the external pressures had fallen off, our field of vision grew broader, and gradually, even if only through a tiny crack, that "whole world" became visible and understandable. To our amazement the "whole world" turned out to be quite different from what we had hoped, it was not living by the "right" values, nor was it headed in the "right" direction; it was a world which upon seeing a slimy bog exclaimed: "What a charming meadow!" and of a concrete pillory said: "What an exquisite necklace!" Where some were shedding tears that could not be wiped away, there others danced to the tune of a carefree musical.

How did this happen? Why this yawning chasm? Were we insensible? Or is the world? Or is this due to a difference in languages? Why are people who address each other sometimes incapable of making out distinct speech? Words ring out and fade away, they flow off like water—leaving no taste, no color, no smell. No trace.

As I came to understand this more and more over the years, a succession of changes was introduced into the structure, meaning, and tone of my projected speech. Today's speech.

And it now bears little resemblance to the one first conceived on those icy evenings in the prison camp.

FOUR

Man has from the beginning been so constituted that his view of the world (if it is not induced by hypnosis), his motivations and scale of values, his actions and his intentions, are all defined by his experience as an individual and as a member of a group. In the words of the Russian proverb: "Your brother, he might lie; trust instead your own bad eye." This is the soundest of bases for understanding one's environment and for acting in it. And for many long centuries, while our world was completely and mysteriously dispersed—before it was interlaced by unbroken lines of communication and turned into a single feverishly throbbing mass —people were unfailingly guided by their own experience within their own circumscribed locality, within their community, within their society, and finally within their national territory. At that time it was possible for the individual human eye to see and accept a certain common scale of values: what was considered average, what unbelievable; what was cruel, what was beyond villainy; what constituted honesty, and what deceit. And even though the scattered nations lived quite differently, and the scales of their social values could diverge as strikingly as their systems of measurement, these discrepancies astonished only the infrequent wayfarer or turned up as curiosities in magazines. They held no danger for humanity, which was not yet united.

But in the course of the last few decades, humanity has imperceptibly and suddenly become united—a unity fraught with hope and with danger—so that shocks or inflammations in one part are instantly passed on to the other portions— some of which may well lack the appropriate immunity. Humanity has become one, but it is not the stable undividedness of a former community or even that of a nation. It is a unity achieved not by means of gradually acquired experience, not from the *eye,* affably referred to as "bad" in the proverb, not even through a common native language; but rather—surmounting all barriers—this is unity brought about by international radio and the press. Onrushing waves of events bear down upon us: half the world learns in one minute of what is splashed ashore. But lacking are the scales or yardsticks to measure these events and to evaluate them according to the laws of the parts of the world unfamiliar to us. Such scales are not, nor can they be, carried to us through the ether or on sheets of newsprint: these scales of values have been settling into place and have been assimilated for too long a time and in too unique a fashion in the particular lives of specific countries and societies; they cannot be transmitted on the wing. In each region men apply to events their own particular hard-won scale of values; intransigently and self-confidently, they judge by their own scale and by no other.

There are perhaps not multitudes of such different yardsticks in the world, but certainly several:

a scale for close-by events and a scale for far-off ones; the scale used by old societies and that used by new ones; the scale of the well off and that of the unfortunate. The gradations on the various scales diverge drastically, their kaleidoscopic variety makes our eyes smart. To prevent discomfort, we dismiss all alien scales out of hand, as if they were madness and error, and we confidently judge the whole world according to our own home-grown scale. Thus we perceive as more significant, more painful, and more intolerable not those conditions which are indeed all these things—but those which are closer to us. But everything that is far away and does not threaten, today, to surge up to our doorsill, we accept—with all its groans, stifled shouts, destroyed lives, and even its millions of victims—as being on the whole quite bearable and of tolerable dimensions.

In one region not so long ago hundreds of thousands of voiceless Christians laid down their lives for their faith in God amid a persecution that yielded nothing to that of ancient Rome. In another hemisphere a certain madman (and he is undoubtedly not alone) speeds across an ocean in order to *free* us from religion with a blade-thrust aimed at the Pontiff. He deduced this from his own scale of values for the benefit of us all.

What according to one scale—from afar—seems an enviable and contented freedom, is perceived according to another scale—close at hand—as galling coercion which calls for buses to be overturned. What in one land would be dreamed of as an improbable level of well-being, in another land provokes resentment as a barbaric exploitation demanding an immediate strike. Different also are the scales for evaluating natural disasters: a flood with two hundred thousand victims seems less important than a minor incident in our home town. There are different scales for assessing personal insult: in one place an ironical smile or a disdainful gesture can humiliate, in others even a cruel beating can be forgiven as a bad joke. There are different scales for punishment and for wrongdoing: according to one, a month-long detention, a banishment to the countryside, or "solitary" with white rolls and milk, all stagger the imagination and fill columns of newsprint with wrath. But according to another scale it is both commonplace and forgivable to have prison sentences of twenty-five years, punishment cells with ice on the walls where the prisoners are stripped to their underwear, insane asylums for normal persons, and shootings at the border of countless unreasonable people who for some reason keep trying to flee somewhere. Our heart is especially at ease about that exotic land about which we know nothing whatsoever, from which no tidings ever reach our ears with the exception of some belated and hackneyed conjectures from a few correspondents.

This double vision, this torpid inability to understand someone else's distant grief, should not be blamed on human eyesight: man is simply built that way. But for mankind as a whole, compressed as it is into a single mass, such a mutual lack of understanding threatens to bring on quick and violent extinction. Given six, four, or even two scales of values, there cannot be a unified world, a united humanity. We shall be torn apart by this difference in rhythm, the divergence in frequency of oscillation. We could not manage to survive on one earth, just as a man with two hearts is not long for this world.

FIVE

But who will reconcile these scales of values and how? Who is going to give mankind a single system of evaluation for evil deeds and for good ones, for unbearable things and for tolerable ones—as we differentiate them today? Who will elucidate for mankind what really is burdensome and unbearable and what merely chafes the skin due to its proximity? Who will direct man's anger toward that which is more fearsome rather than toward that which is closer at hand? Who could convey this understanding across the barriers of his own human experience? Who could impress upon a sluggish and obstinate human being someone else's far-off sorrows or joys, who could give him an insight into magnitudes of events and into delusions which he has never himself experienced? Propaganda, coercion, and scientific proof are all equally powerless here. But fortunately there does exist a means to this end in the world! It is art. It is literature.

They both hold the key to a miracle: to overcome man's ruinous habit of learning only from his own experience, so that the experience of others passes him by without profit. Making up for man's scant time on earth, art transmits between men the entire accumulated load of another being's life experience, with all its hardships, colors, and juices. It recreates—lifelike—the experience of other men, so that we can assimilate it as our own.

But even more, much more than this: countries and entire continents continually repeat each other's mistakes with a time lag—occasionally one of centuries—when, it would seem, everything is so very clear. But no: what one people has already endured, appraised, and rejected suddenly emerges among another people as the very latest word. Here once again the sole substitute for an experience which we have not ourselves lived through is art and literature. Both are endowed with the miraculous power to communicate—despite differences in language, custom, and social structure—the experience of the entire nation to another nation which has not undergone such a difficult decades-long collective experience. In a fortunate instance, this could save an entire nation from a redundant, or erroneous, or even destructive course, thereby shortening the tortuous paths of human history.

It is this great and blessed property of art to which I resolutely wish to call attention today from this Nobel platform.

There is one other invaluable direction in which literature transmits incontrovertible condensed experience: from generation to generation. In this way literature becomes the living memory of a nation. It sustains within itself and safeguards a nation's bygone history—in a form which cannot be distorted or falsified. In this way does literature together with language preserve the national soul.

(It has lately been fashionable to speak of the leveling of nations, of the disappearance of individual peoples in the melting pot of modern civilization. I disagree, but a discussion of this problem would be a theme in itself. It is here appropriate to say only that the disappearance of nations would impoverish us not less than if all men should become alike, with one personality and one face. Nations are the wealth of mankind, its generalized personalities; the least among them has its own unique coloration and harbors within itself a unique facet of God's design.)

But woe to that nation whose literature is cut short by the intrusion of force. This is not merely interference with "freedom of the press" but the sealing up of a nation's heart, the excision of its memory. A nation can no longer remember itself, it loses its spiritual unity, and despite their seemingly common language, countrymen cease to understand one another. Mute generations live out their lives and die, without giving an account of their experiences either to themselves or to their descendants. When such literary masters as Akhmatova or Zamyatin are walled up for their entire lives, condemned till the grave to create in silence and unable to hear any echoes to their work—then this is not only their personal misfortune, but a calamity for the whole nation, a menace to it.

And in some cases this could even be a grievous misfortune for the whole of humanity: whenever such silence causes all of *history* to become incomprehensible.

SIX

At various times and in various countries there have been heated, angry, and refined polemics about whether art and the artist should live for their own sake or whether they must always keep in mind their duty toward society and serve it, albeit without bias. For me the answer is obvious, but I shall not once again rehearse the long train of arguments. One of the most brilliant statements on this theme was Albert Camus's Nobel Lecture, and I happily join in his conclusions. Indeed, Russian literature has for decades been disinclined to engage in excessive self-contemplation, or in flitting about in too carefree a manner—and I am not ashamed to continue this tradition to the best of my ability. Through Russian literature we have long ago grown familiar with the concept that a writer can do much among his people—and that he must.

We shall not trample on the *right* of an artist to express nothing but his personal experiences and his self-observations while disregarding all that occurs in the rest of the world. We shall not make *demands* on him—but surely we can be permitted to reproach him, beg him, call him, or beckon to him. After all, an artist develops his gift only partially by himself; the greater part has been breathed into him ready-made at birth. And together with this talent, a responsibility has been imposed upon his free will. Granted, an artist does not *owe* anything to anyone, but it is painful to see how, by withdrawing into self-created worlds or into the realms of subjective whim, he *can* surrender the real world into the hands of profit-seekers, of nonentities, or even of madmen.

This twentieth century of ours has proved to be crueler than its predecessors, and its horrors have not been exhausted with the end of its first half. The same old atavistic urges—greed, envy, unrestrained passion, and mutual hostility—readily picking up respectable pseudonyms like class, race, mass, or trade union struggle, claw at and tear apart our world. A primitive rejection of all compromise is given the status of a theoretical principle and is regarded as the high virtue which accompanies doctrinal purity. This attitude creates millions of victims in ceaseless civil wars, it drones into our souls that there exist no lasting concepts of good and justice valid for all mankind, that all such concepts are fluid and ever changing —which is why you should always act in a way that benefits your party. Any professional group, at the first opportunity to *get their hand on something extra*—though unearned and even unneeded— grabs it, and the rest of society be damned. As seen from the outside, the careening fluctuations of Western society seem to be approaching that amplitude beyond which a system becomes metastable and must disintegrate. Less and less restrained by the confines of long-established legality, violence strides brazenly and triumphantly through the world, unconcerned that its futility has already been demonstrated and proven many times in history. It is not even brute force alone that is victorious, but also its clamorous justification: the world is being flooded by the brazen conviction that force can do all, and righteousness—nothing. Dostoyevsky's *Devils,* who had seemed part of a provincial nightmarish fantasy of the last century, are now infesting the world before our eyes, reaching lands where they could not earlier have even been imagined. And now, by the hijacking of airplanes, by the seizing of hostages, by the explosions and conflagrations of recent years, they signal their determination to shake civilization to its roots and to bring it down. And they may well succeed. Today's youth, at an age when they have not yet had any experience except sex, before they have lived through their own years of suffering and reached their own personal understanding—these young people enthusiastically mouth the discredited clichés of the Russian nineteenth century, thinking that they are uncovering something new. The recently manifested degradation of human beings into nonentities as practiced by the Chinese Red Guards is taken as a joyous model by the young. What shallow lack of understanding of timeless human nature, what naïve confidence of inexperienced hearts: "We'll just oust *these* vicious, greedy oppressors and rulers, and those next in charge (that's us!), having put aside grenades and submachine guns, will be compassionate and just." Some chance indeed! . . . And yet among those who have seen life, who do understand, and who could refute these young people—many *do not dare* to do so. They even assume fawning attitudes, just so as not to seem "conservative." This once again is a Russian nineteenth-century phenomenon; Dostoyevsky called it *subservience to progressive little notions.*

The spirit of Munich has by no means retreated into the past, it was no short-lived episode. I would even dare to claim that the spirit of Munich dominates the twentieth century. A timorous civilized world, faced with the onslaught of a suddenly revived and snarling barbarism, has found nothing to oppose it with except concessions and smiles. The spirit of Munich is a malady of the will of affluent people; it is the chronic state of those who have abandoned themselves to a pursuit of prosperity at any price, who have succumbed to a belief in material well-being as the principal goal of life on earth. Such people—and there are many in today's world—choose passivity and retreat, just so long as their accustomed life can be made to last a little longer, just so long as the transition to hardship can be put off for another day; and tomorrow —who knows?—everything may turn out to be all right. (But it never will! The price paid for cowardice will only be the more exorbitant. Courage and victory come to us only when we are resolved to make sacrifices.)

We are also threatened by destruction from another quarter: our physically compressed and cramped world is restrained from merging spiritually; molecules of knowledge and sympathy are prevented from leaping from one half to the other. This *blockage of information flow* between parts of the planet is a mortal danger. Modern science knows that the blockage of information is the way of entropy and of general destruction. Information blockage renders illusory international agreements and treaties: within the *isolated* zone there is nothing easier than to reinterpret any treaty or simply to forget it as if it had never existed (Orwell understood this well). This isolated zone seems to be inhabited not by earthlings but by some expeditionary force from Mars; these people know nothing about the rest of the earth and are ready to trample it underfoot in the solemn belief that they are "liberating" it.

A quarter of a century ago the United Nations Organization was born amid the great hopes of mankind. But alas, in an immoral world it too grew up without morality. It is not a United Nations Organization but a United Governments Organization, where governments freely elected are equated with regimes imposed by force or with those that have gained control by an armed seizure of power. By dint of the self-interested bias of the majority of its members, the UN jealously guards the freedom of certain peoples and completely neglects the freedom of others. Through an obeisant vote it has rejected the investigation of *private grievances*—the moans, cries, and entreaties of humble individual *mere people,* who were judged entities just too minuscule for such a great organization. Its best document in the twenty-five years of its existence—the Universal Declaration of Human Rights—the UN has not taken the trouble to make *mandatory* for its member governments, a *condition* of membership, and has thereby abandoned little people to the mercy of governments they did not elect.

One might have thought that the structure of the modern world would be entirely in the hands of scientists, since it is they who decide all the technical steps of mankind. One might have thought that the direction in which the world is to move would be determined by a worldwide concord of scientists, not of politicians. All the more so since the example of individuals demonstrates how much ground they could gain if only they joined forces. But no: scientists have made no explicit attempts to become an important, independently motivated force within mankind. Entire congresses of them back away from the suffering of others: it is cozier to remain within the limits of science. The same spirit of Munich has spread its enervating wings over them.

What, then—in this cruel, dynamic, explosive world which totters on the brink of destruction—what *is* the place and role of the writer? We do not, after all, send up rockets, we don't even push the meanest of supply carts. Indeed, we are held in total contempt by those who respect material might alone. Would it not be natural for us also to retreat, to lose faith in the unshakable nature of goodness, in the indivisible nature of truth? Should not we merely recite to the world our bitter but detached observations about how hopelessly warped mankind is, how shallow people have become, and how burdensome it is for a lone refined and beautiful soul to dwell among them?

But even this escape is not open to us. Once we have taken up the *word,* it is thereafter impossible to turn away: a writer is no detached judge of his countrymen and contemporaries; he is an accomplice to all the evil committed in his country or by his people. And if the tanks of his fatherland have bloodied the pavement of a foreign capital, then rust-colored stains have forever bespattered the writer's face. And if on some fateful night a trusting friend is strangled in his sleep—then the palms of the writer bear the bruises from that rope. And if his youthful fellow citizens nonchalantly proclaim the advantages of debauchery over humble toil, if they abandon themselves to drugs, or seize hostages—then this stench too is mingled with the breath of the writer.

Have we the insolence to declare that we do not answer for the evils of today's world?

SEVEN

But I am encouraged by a vivid sense of *world literature* as one great heart which beats for the cares and woes of our world, though each of these is manifested and perceived in its own way in its separate corner of the globe.

Apart from the well-established tradition of national literatures, there has long existed the concept of world literature. It was traditionally seen as a curve enveloping the peaks of the national literatures and as the sum total of all literary influences. But there were time lags: readers and writers discovered foreign authors with a delay, occasionally one of centuries. As a result, mutual influences were held back and the curve encompassing the national literary high points was discerned only by posterity, not by contemporaries.

But today there exists an interaction between the writers of one land and the writers and readers of other lands which, though not immediate, is close to it; I can vouch for this myself. My books—unpublished, alas, in my own country—have in spite of hasty and often poor translations rapidly acquired a responsive world readership. Outstanding Western writers such as Heinrich Böll have devoted critical analyses to them. Throughout these last years, when my work and my freedom did not collapse, when they seemed to hang in midair in violation of the laws of gravity, seemingly supported by *nothing at all*—except the invisible and mute tension of the cohesive film of public sympathy—all those years I have gratefully and quite unexpectedly come to know the support of the worldwide brotherhood of writers. On my fiftieth birthday I was astounded to receive congratulations from well-known European writers. No pressure upon me could any longer pass unnoticed. In the hazardous weeks when I was being expelled from the Union of Writers, the *protective wall* erected by the writers of the world saved me from worse persecution, while Norwegian writers and artists hospitably readied a shelter for me in case the threatened banishment from my homeland should occur. Finally, my very nomination for the Nobel Prize was initiated not in the country where I live and work, but by François Mauriac and his colleagues. And more recently still, entire organizations of national writers have expressed their support for me.

And so I came to understand through my own experience that world literature is no longer an abstract enveloping curve, no longer a generalization coined by literary scholars, but a kind of collective body and a common spirit, a living unity of the heart which reflects the growing spiritual unity of mankind. Borders of states continue to turn crimson, heated to a red glow by electrified wire and by bursts of machine gun fire. Certain ministries of internal affairs continue to believe that literature too is an "internal affair" of the countries over which they claim jurisdiction. Newspapers continue to display banner headlines: "They have no right to interfere in our internal affairs!" But in the meantime—all *internal affairs* have ceased to exist on our crowded earth! The salvation of mankind lies only in making everything the concern of all. People in the East should without exception be concerned with what people are thinking in the West; people in the West should without exception care about what is happening in the East. Literature, one of the most sophisticated and sensitive instruments available to human beings, has been one of the first to pick up, to assimilate, and to join in expressing this feeling of the growing unity of mankind. And I here confidently address myself to the world literature of today—to the hundreds of friends whom I have never met in person and whom I perhaps may never see.

Friends! Let us try to help if we are worth anything at all! Who in our various countries—torn as they are by the tumultuous discord of parties, movements, castes, and groups—who is it that from the beginning has been not a divisive force but a unifying one? That, in essence, is the role of writers: they are the articulators of the national tongue (that main tie which holds a nation together) and of the very land inhabited by a people; in fortunate instances, they give expression to the national soul.

I believe that world literature is fully capable of helping a troubled humanity to recognize its true self in spite of what is advocated by biased individuals and parties. World literature is capable of transmitting the concentrated experience of a particular region to other lands so that we can overcome double vision and kaleidoscopic variety, so that one people can discover, accurately and concisely, the true history of another people, with all the force of recognition and the pain that comes from actual experience—and can thus be safeguarded from belated errors. And at the same time we ourselves shall perhaps be able to develop a *world vision:* focusing on what is close at hand with the center of our eye—just like everyone else —we shall begin to use our peripheral vision to take in what occurs in the rest of the world. And we shall proceed to make correlations, adhering to a worldwide standard.

Who else but writers shall condemn their incompetent rulers (in some states this is in fact the easiest way to earn a living; it is done by anyone who feels the urge), who else shall censure their respective societies—be it for cowardly submission or for self-satisfied weakness—as well as the witless excesses of the young and the youthful pirates with knives upraised?

We shall be told: What can literature do in the face of a remorseless assault of open violence? But let us not forget that violence does not and cannot exist by itself: it is invariably intertwined with *the lie*. They are linked in the most intimate, most organic and profound fashion: violence cannot conceal itself behind anything except lies, and lies have nothing to maintain them save violence. Anyone who has once proclaimed violence as his *method* must inexorably choose the lie as his *principle*. At birth, violence acts openly and even takes pride in itself. But as soon as it gains strength and becomes firmly established, it begins to sense the air around it growing thinner; it can no longer exist without veiling itself in a mist of lies, without concealing itself behind the sugary words of false-hood. No longer does violence always and neces-sarily lunge straight for your throat; more often than not it demands of its subjects only that they pledge allegiance to lies, that they participate in falsehood.

The simple act of an ordinary brave man is not to participate in lies, not to support false actions! His rule: let *that* come into the world, let it even reign supreme—only not through me. But it is within the power of writers and artists to do much more: *to defeat the lie!* For in the struggle with lies art has always triumphed and shall always tri-umph! Visibly, irrefutably for all! Lies can prevail against much in this world, but never against art.

And no sooner will the lies be dispersed than the repulsive nakedness of violence will be exposed—and age-old violence will topple in defeat.

This is why I believe, my friends, that we are capable of helping the world in its hour of crisis. We should not seek to justify our unwillingness by our lack of weapons, nor should we give ourselves up to a life of comfort. We must come out and join the battle!

The favorite proverbs in Russian are about *truth*. They forcefully express a long and difficult national experience, sometimes in striking fashion:

One word of truth shall outweigh the whole world.

It is on such a seemingly fantastic violation of the law of conservation of mass and energy that my own activity is based, and my appeal to the writers of the world.

A WORLD SPLIT APART

COMMENCEMENT ADDRESS

DELIVERED

AT HARVARD UNIVERSITY

JUNE 8, 1978

Translated from the Russian
by Irina Ilovayskaya Alberti

I am sincerely happy to be here with you on the occasion of the 327th commencement of this old and illustrious university. My congratulations and best wishes to all of today's graduates.

Harvard's motto is "Veritas." Many of you have already discovered and others will learn in the course of their lives that truth eludes us as soon as our concentration begins to flag, all the while leaving the illusion that we are continuing to pursue it. This is the source of much discord. Furthermore, truth seldom is sweet; it is almost invariably bitter. A measure of bitter truth is included in my speech today, but I offer it as a friend, not as an adversary.

Three years ago in the United States I said certain things that were rejected and appeared unacceptable. Today, however, many people agree with what I then said. . . .

A WORLD SPLIT APART

The split in today's world is perceptible even to a hasty glance. Anyone living today can easily distinguish two world powers, each of them already capable of utterly destroying the other. However, the understanding of the split is too often limited to this political conception: the illusion according to which the danger may be eliminated through successful diplomatic negotiations or by achieving a military balance. The truth is that the split is both more profound and more alienating and that the fissures are more numerous than one can see at first glance. This deep and multiform split threatens us all with an equally manifold disaster, in accordance with the ancient truth that a kingdom—in this case, our earth—divided against itself cannot stand.

CONTEMPORARY WORLDS

There is the concept of the Third World: thus, we already have three worlds. Undoubtedly, however, the number is even greater; we are just too far away to see. Every ancient and deeply rooted self-contained culture, especially if it is spread over a wide part of the earth's surface, constitutes a self-contained world, full of riddles and surprises to Western thinking. As a minimum, we must include in this category China, India, the Muslim world, and Africa, if indeed we accept the approximation of viewing the latter two as uniform. For one thousand years Russia belonged to such a category, although Western thinking systematically committed the mistake of denying its special character and therefore never understood it, just as today the West does not understand Russia in Communist captivity. And while it may be that in past years Japan has increasingly become, in effect, a Far West, drawing ever closer to Western ways (I am no judge here), Israel, I think, should not be reckoned as part of the West, if only because of the decisive circumstance that its state system is fundamentally linked to religion.

Only a short time ago, relatively, the small world of modern Europe had easily seized colonies all over the globe, not only without anticipating any real resistance, but usually with contempt for any possible values in the conquered peoples' approach to life. It all seemed an overwhelming success, with no geographic limits. Western society presented the triumph of human independence and power. But suddenly the twentieth century brought the clear realization of this society's fragility. We now see that the conquests proved to be short-lived and precarious (and this, in turn, points to defects in the Western view of the world which led to these conquests). Relations with the former colonial world now have switched to the opposite extreme and the Western world often exhibits an excess of obsequiousness, but it is difficult to estimate the size of the bill which former colonial countries will present to the West and to predict whether the surrender not only of its last colonies, but of everything it owns, will be sufficient for the West to clear this account.

CONVERGENCE

But the persisting blindness of superiority continues to hold that all the vast regions of our planet should seek the level of development of contemporary Western systems, the best in theory and the most attractive in practice; that all these other worlds are but temporarily prevented (by wicked leaders or by severe crises or by their own barbarity and incomprehension) from pursuing Western pluralistic democracy and adopting the Western way of life. Countries are judged according to their progress in that direction. But in fact such a conception is a fruit of Western incomprehension of the essence of other worlds, a result of mistakenly measuring them all with a Western yardstick. The real picture of our planet's development bears little resemblance to all this.

The anguish of a divided world gave birth to the theory of convergence between the leading Western countries and the Soviet Union. It is a soothing theory which overlooks the fact that these worlds are not at all evolving toward each other and that neither one can be transformed into the other without violence. Besides, convergence inevitably means acceptance of the other side's defects, and this can hardly suit anyone.

If I were today addressing an audience in my country, I would have concentrated on the calamities of the East in my examination of the overall pattern of the world's rifts. But since my forced exile in the West has now lasted four years and since my audience is a Western one, I think it may be of greater interest to concentrate on certain aspects of the contemporary West, such as I see them.

A DECLINE IN COURAGE

A decline in courage may be the most striking feature that an outside observer notices in the West today. The Western world has lost its civic courage, both as a whole and separately, in each country, in each government, in each political party, and, of course, in the United Nations. Such a decline in courage is particularly noticeable among the ruling and intellectual elites, causing an impression of a loss of courage by the entire society. There of course remain many courageous individuals, but they have no determining influence on public life. Political and intellectual functionaries exhibit this depression, passivity, and perplexity in their actions and in their statements, and even more so in their self-serving rationales as to how realistic, reasonable, and intellectually and even morally justified it is to base state policies on weakness and cowardice. And the decline in courage, at times attaining what could be termed a lack of manhood, is ironically emphasized by occasional outbursts of boldness and inflexibility on the part of those same functionaries when dealing with weak governments and with countries that lack support, or with doomed currents which clearly cannot offer any resistance. But they get tongue-tied and paralyzed when they deal with powerful governments and threatening forces, with aggressors and international terrorists.

Must one point out that from ancient times a decline in courage has been considered the first symptom of the end?

WELL-BEING

When the modern Western states were being formed, it was proclaimed as a principle that governments are meant to serve man and that man lives in order to be free and pursue happiness. (See, for example, the American Declaration of Independence.) Now, at last, the technical and social progress of recent years has permitted the realization of such aspirations: the welfare state. Every citizen has been granted the desired freedom and material goods in such quantity and of such quality as to guarantee in theory the achievement of happiness, in the debased sense of the word which has come into being during those same decades. (In the process, however, one psychological detail has been overlooked: the constant desire to have still more things and a still better life; the struggle to this end imprints many Western faces with worry and even depression, though it is customary to conceal such feelings carefully. This active and tense competition comes to dominate all human thought and does not in the least give rise to free spiritual development.) The individual's independence from many types of state pressure has been guaranteed; the majority of the people have been provided with comforts of a kind their fathers and grandfathers could not even have imagined; it has become possible to raise young people according to these ideals, preparing them for and summoning them toward physical well-being, happiness, the possession of material goods, money, and leisure, toward an almost unlimited freedom in the choice of pleasures. So who should now renounce all this, why and for the sake of what should one risk one's precious life in defense of the common good and particularly in the nebulous case when the security of one's nation must be defended in an as yet distant land?

Even biology tells us that a high degree of habitual well-being is not advantageous to a living organism. Today, well-being in the life of Western society has begun to take off its pernicious mask.

LEGALISTIC LIFE

Western society has chosen for itself the type of existence best suited to its purposes and one I would call legalistic. The limits of human rights and rightness are defined by a system of laws; such limits are very broad. People in the West have acquired considerable skill in using, interpreting, and manipulating law (though laws tend to be too complicated for an average person to understand without the help of an expert). Every conflict is solved according to the letter of the law and this is considered to be the ultimate solution. If one is right from a legal point of view, nothing more is required; nobody may mention that one could still not be entirely right, and urge self-restraint or a renunciation of these rights, call for sacrifice and selfless risk: this would simply sound absurd. Voluntary self-restraint is almost unheard of: everybody strives toward further expansion to the extreme limit of the legal frames. (An oil company is legally blameless when it buys up an invention of a new type of energy in order to prevent its use. A food product manufacturer is legally blameless when he poisons his produce to make it last longer: after all, people are free not to purchase it.)

I have spent all my life under a Communist regime and I will tell you that a society without any objective legal scale is a terrible one indeed. But a society with no other scale but the legal one is also less than worthy of man. A society based on the letter of the law and never reaching any higher fails to take advantage of the full range of human possibilities. The letter of the law is too cold and formal to have a beneficial influence on society. Whenever the tissue of life is woven of legalistic relationships, this creates an atmosphere of spiritual mediocrity that paralyzes man's noblest impulses.

And it will be simply impossible to bear up to the trials of this threatening century with nothing but the supports of a legalistic structure.

THE DIRECTION OF FREEDOM

Today's Western society has revealed the inequality between the freedom for good deeds and the freedom for evil deeds. A statesman who wants to achieve something important and highly constructive for his country has to move cautiously and even timidly; thousands of hasty (and irresponsible) critics cling to him at all times; he is constantly rebuffed by parliament and the press. He has to prove that his every step is well-founded and absolutely flawless. Indeed, an outstanding, truly great person who has unusual and unexpected initiatives in mind does not get any chance to assert himself; dozens of traps will be set for him from the beginning. Thus mediocrity triumphs under the guise of democratic restraints.

It is feasible and easy everywhere to undermine administrative power and it has in fact been drastically weakened in all Western countries. The defense of individual rights has reached such extremes as to make society as a whole defenseless against certain individuals. It is time, in the West, to uphold not so much human rights as human obligations.

On the other hand, destructive and irresponsible freedom has been granted boundless scope. Society has turned out to be poorly defended against the abyss of human decadence, for example against the misuse of liberty for moral violence against young people, such as motion pictures full of pornography, crime, and horror. This is all considered to be part of freedom and to be counterbalanced, in theory, by the young people's right not to look and not to accept. Life organized legalistically has thus shown its inability to defend itself against the corrosion of evil.

And what shall we say about the dark realms of overt criminality? Legal limits (especially in the United States) are broad enough to encourage not only individual freedom but also some misuse of such freedom. The culprit can go unpunished or obtain undeserved leniency—all with the support of thousands of defenders in the society. When a government earnestly undertakes to root out terrorism, public opinion immediately accuses it of violating the terrorists' civil rights. There are quite a number of such cases.

This tilt of freedom toward evil has come about gradually, but it evidently stems from a humanistic and benevolent concept according to which man—the master of this world—does not bear any evil within himself, and all the defects of life are caused by misguided social systems, which must therefore be corrected. Yet strangely enough, though the best social conditions have been achieved in the West, there still remains a great deal of crime; there even is considerably more of it than in the destitute and lawless Soviet society. (There is a multitude of prisoners in our camps who are termed criminals, but most of them never committed any crime; they merely tried to defend themselves against a lawless state by resorting to means outside the available legal framework.)

THE DIRECTION OF THE PRESS

The press too, of course, enjoys the widest freedom. (I shall be using the word "press" to include all the media.) But what use does it make of it?

Here again, the overriding concern is not to infringe the letter of the law. There is no true moral responsibility for distortion or disproportion. What sort of responsibility does a journalist or a newspaper have to the readership or to history? If they have misled public opinion by inaccurate information or wrong conclusions, even if they have contributed to mistakes on a state level, do we know of any case of open regret voiced by the same journalist or the same newspaper? No; this would damage sales. A nation may be the worse for such a mistake, but the journalist always gets away with it. It is most likely that he will start writing the exact opposite to his previous statements with renewed aplomb.

The need to provide instant and credible-sounding information leads to the practice of filling lacunae with guesses, collecting rumors and suppositions, none of which will ever be refuted but will settle into the readers' memory. How many hasty, immature, superficial, and misleading judgments are expressed every day, confusing readers, and are then left hanging? The press also has the ability to simulate public opinion or to miseducate it. Thus we may see terrorists heroized, or secret matters pertaining to the nation's defense publicly revealed, or we may witness shameless intrusion into the privacy of well-known people according to the slogan "Everyone is entitled to know everything." (But this is a false slogan of a false era; far greater in value is the forfeited right of people *not to know*, not to have their divine souls stuffed with gossip, nonsense, vain talk. A person whose life and work are meaningful has no need for this excessive and burdening flow of information.)

Hastiness and superficiality—these are the psychic diseases of the twentieth century and more than anywhere else these are manifested in the press. In-depth analysis of a problem is anathema to the press; it is contrary to its nature. The press merely picks out sensational formulas.

Such as it is, however, the press has become the greatest power within the Western countries, exceeding that of the legislature, the executive, and the judiciary. Yet one would like to ask: According to what law has it been elected and to whom is it responsible? In the Communist East, a journalist is frankly appointed as a state official. But who has voted Western journalists into their positions of power, for how long a time, and with what prerogatives?

There is yet another surprise for someone coming from the totalitarian East with its rigorously unified press: One discovers a common trend of preferences within the Western press as a whole (the spirit of the times), generally accepted patterns of judgment, and maybe common corporate interests, the sum effect being not competition but unification. Unrestrained freedom exists for the press, but not for the readership, because newspapers mostly transmit in a forceful and emphatic way those opinions which do not too openly contradict their own and that general trend.

A FASHION IN THINKING

Without any censorship in the West, fashionable trends of thought and ideas are fastidiously separated from those that are not fashionable, and the latter, without ever being forbidden, have little chance of finding their way into periodicals or books or being heard in colleges. Your scholars are free in the legal sense, but they are hemmed in by the idols of the prevailing fad. There is no open violence, as in the East; however, a selection dictated by fashion and the need to accommodate mass standards frequently prevents the most independent-minded persons from contributing to public life and gives rise to dangerous herd instincts that block successful development. In America, I have received letters from highly intelligent persons—maybe a teacher in a faraway small college who could do much for the renewal and salvation of his country, but the country cannot hear him because the media will not provide him with a forum. This gives birth to strong mass prejudices, to a blindness which is perilous in our dynamic era. An example is the self-deluding interpretation of the state of affairs in the contemporary world that functions as a sort of a petrified armor around people's minds, to such a degree that human voices from seventeen countries of Eastern Europe and Eastern Asia cannot pierce it. It will be broken only by the inexorable crowbar of events.

I have mentioned a few traits of Western life which surprise and shock a new arrival to this world. The purpose and scope of this speech will not allow me to continue such a survey, in particular to look into the impact of these characteristics on important aspects of a nation's life, such as elementary education, advanced education in the humanities, and art.

SOCIALISM

It is almost universally recognized that the West shows all the world the way to successful economic development, even though in past years it has been sharply offset by chaotic inflation. However, many people living in the West are dissatisfied with their own society. They despise it or accuse it of no longer being up to the level of maturity attained by mankind. And this causes many to be swayed toward socialism, which is a false and dangerous current.

I hope that no one present will suspect me of expressing my partial criticism of the Western system in order to suggest socialism as an alternative. No; with the experience of a country where socialism has been realized, I shall certainly not speak for such an alternative. The mathematician Igor Shafarevich, a member of the Soviet Academy of Science, has written a brilliantly argued book entitled *The Socialist Phenomenon;* this is a penetrating historical analysis demonstrating that socialism of any type and shade leads to a total destruction of the human spirit and to a leveling of mankind into death. Shafarevich's book was published in France almost two years ago and so far no one has been found to refute it. It will shortly be published in English in the United States.

NOT A MODEL

But should I be asked, instead, whether I would propose the West, such as it is today, as a model to my country, I would frankly have to answer negatively. No, I could not recommend your society as an ideal for the transformation of ours. Through deep suffering, people in our country have now achieved a spiritual development of such intensity that the Western system in its present state of spiritual exhaustion does not look attractive. Even those characteristics of your life which I have just enumerated are extremely saddening.

A fact which cannot be disputed is the weakening of human personality in the West while in the East it has become firmer and stronger. Six decades have passed for our people, three for the people of Eastern Europe; during that time we have been through a spiritual training far in advance of Western experience. The complex and deadly crush of life has produced stronger, deeper, and more interesting personalities than those generated by standardized Western well-being. Therefore, if our society were to be transformed into yours, it would mean an improvement in certain aspects, but also a change for the worse on some particularly significant points. Of course, a society cannot remain in an abyss of lawlessness, as is the case in our country. But it is also demeaning for it to stay on such a soulless and smooth plane of legalism, as in the case in yours. After the suffering of decades of violence and oppression, the human soul longs for things higher, warmer, and purer than those offered by today's mass living habits, introduced as by a calling card by the revolting invasion of commercial advertising, by TV stupor, and by intolerable music.

All this is visible to numerous observers from all the worlds of our planet. The Western way of life is less and less likely to become the leading model.

There are telltale symptoms by which history gives warning to a threatened or perishing society. Such are, for instance, a decline of the arts or a lack of great statesmen. Indeed, sometimes the warnings are quite explicit and concrete. The center of your democracy and of your culture is left without electric power for a few hours only, and suddenly crowds of American citizens start looting and creating havoc. The smooth surface film must be very thin, then, the social system quite unstable and unhealthy.

But the fight for our planet, physical and spiritual, a fight of cosmic proportions, is not a vague matter of the future; it has already started. The forces of Evil have begun their decisive offensive. You can feel their pressure, yet your screens and publications are full of prescribed smiles and raised glasses. What is the joy about?

SHORT-SIGHTEDNESS

Very well known representatives of your society, such as George Kennan, say: We cannot apply moral criteria to politics. Thus we mix good and evil, right and wrong, and make room for the absolute triumph of absolute evil in the world. Only moral criteria can help the West against communism's well-planned world strategy. There are no other criteria. Practical or occasional considerations of any kind will inevitably be swept away by strategy. After a certain level of the problem has been reached, legalistic thinking induces paralysis; it prevents one from seeing the scale and the meaning of events.

In spite of the abundance of information, or maybe partly because of it, the West has great difficulty in finding its bearings amid contemporary events. There have been naïve predictions by some American experts who believed that Angola would become the Soviet Union's Vietnam or that the impudent Cuban expeditions in Africa would best be stopped by special U.S. courtesy to Cuba. Kennan's advice to his own country—to begin unilateral disarmament—belongs to the same category. If you only knew how the youngest of the officials in Moscow's Old Square* roar with laughter at your political wizards! As to Fidel Castro, he openly scorns the United States, boldly sending his troops to distant adventures from his country right next to yours.

However, the most cruel mistake occurred with the failure to understand the Vietnam War. Some people sincerely wanted all wars to stop just as soon as possible; others believed that the way should be left open for national, or Communist, self-determination in Vietnam (or in Cambodia, as we see today with particular clarity). But in fact, members of the U.S. antiwar movement became

*The Old Square in Moscow *(Staraya Ploshchad)* is the place where the headquarters of the Central Committee of the CPSU are located; it is the real name of what in the West is conventionally referred to as the Kremlin.

accomplices in the betrayal of Far Eastern nations, in the genocide and the suffering today imposed on thirty million people there. Do these convinced pacifists now hear the moans coming from there? Do they understand their responsibility today? Or do they prefer not to hear? The American intelligentsia lost its nerve and as a consequence the danger has come much closer to the United States. But there is no awareness of this. Your short-sighted politician who signed the hasty Vietnam capitulation seemingly gave America a carefree breathing pause; however, a hundredfold Vietnam now looms over you. Small Vietnam had been a warning and an occasion to mobilize the nation's courage. But if the full might of America suffered a full-fledged defeat at the hands of a small Communist half-country, how can the West hope to stand firm in the future?

I have said on another occasion that in the twentieth century Western democracy has not won any major war by itself; each time it shielded itself with an ally possessing a powerful land army, whose philosophy it did not question. In World War II against Hitler, instead of winning the conflict with its own forces, which would certainly have been sufficient, Western democracy raised up another enemy, one that would prove worse and more powerful, since Hitler had neither the resources nor the people, nor the ideas with broad appeal, nor such a large number of supporters in the West—a fifth column—as the Soviet Union possessed. Some Western voices already have spoken of the need of a protective screen against hostile forces in the next world conflict; in this case, the shield would be China. But I would not wish such an outcome to any country in the world. First of all, it is again a doomed alliance with evil; it would grant the United States a respite, but when at a later date China with its billion people would turn around armed with American weapons, America itself would fall victim to a Cambodia-style genocide.

LOSS OF WILL

And yet no weapons, no matter how powerful, can help the West until it overcomes its loss of will power. In a state of psychological weakness, weapons even become a burden for the capitulating side. To defend oneself, one must also be ready to die; there is little such readiness in a society raised in the cult of material well-being. Nothing is left, in this case, but concessions, attempts to gain time, and betrayal. Thus at the shameful Belgrade conference, free Western diplomats in their weakness 'surrendered the line of defense for which enslaved members of the Helsinki Watch Groups are sacrificing their lives.

Western thinking has become conservative: the world situation must stay as it is at any cost; there must be no changes. This debilitating dream of a status quo is the symptom of a society that has ceased to develop. But one must be blind in order not to see that the oceans no longer belong to the West, while the land under its domination keeps shrinking. The two so-called world wars (they were by far not on a world scale, not yet) constituted the internal self-destruction of the small progressive West which has thus prepared its own end. The next war (which does not have to be an atomic one; I do not believe it will be) may well bury Western civilization forever.

In the face of such a danger, with such historical values in your past, with such a high level of attained freedom and, apparently, of devotion to it, how is it possible to lose to such an extent the will to defend oneself?

HUMANISM AND ITS CONSEQUENCES

How has this unfavorable relation of forces come about? How did the West decline from its triumphal march to its present debility? Have there been fatal turns and losses of direction in its development? It does not seem so. The West kept advancing steadily in accordance with its proclaimed social intentions, hand in hand with a dazzling progress in technology. And suddenly it found itself in its present state of weakness.

This means that the mistake must be at the root, at the very foundation of thought in modern times. I refer to the prevailing Western view of the world which arose in the Renaissance and has found political expression since the Age of Enlightenment. It became the basis for political and social doctrine and could be called rationalistic humanism or humanistic autonomy: the principle, proclaimed in theory and followed in practice, of man's autonomy from any higher force above him. It could also be called anthropocentricity, with man seen as the center of all.

The shift introduced by the Renaissance was probably inevitable historically: the Middle Ages had come to a natural end by exhaustion, having become an intolerable despotic repression of man's physical nature in favor of the spiritual one. But then we recoiled from the spirit and embraced all that is material, excessively and incommensurately. The humanistic way of thinking, which had proclaimed itself our guide, did not admit the existence of intrinsic evil in man, nor did it see any task higher than the attainment of happiness on earth. It started modern Western civilization on the dangerous trend of worshiping man and his material needs. Everything beyond physical well-being and the accumulation of material goods, all other human requirements and characteristics of a subtler and higher nature, were left outside the area of attention of state and social systems, as if human life did not have any higher meaning. Thus gaps were left open for evil, and its drafts blow freely today. Mere freedom per se does not in the least solve all the problems of human life and even adds a number of new ones.

And yet in early democracies, as in American democracy at the time of its birth, all individual human rights were granted on the ground that man is God's creature. That is, freedom was given to the individual conditionally, in the assumption of his constant religious responsibility. Such was the heritage of the preceding one thousand years. Two hundred or even fifty years ago, it would have seemed quite impossible, in America, that an individual be granted boundless freedom with no purpose, simply for the satisfaction of his whims. Subsequently, however, all such limitations were eroded everywhere in the West; a total emancipation occurred from the moral heritage of the Christian centuries with their great reserves of mercy and sacrifice. State systems were becoming ever more materialistic. The West has finally achieved the rights of man, and even to excess, but man's sense of responsibility to God and society has grown dimmer and dimmer. In the past decades, the legalistic selfishness of the Western approach to the world has reached its peak and the world has found itself in a harsh spiritual crisis and a political impasse. All the celebrated technological achievements of progress, including the conquest of outer space, do not redeem the twentieth century's moral poverty, which no one could have imagined even as recently as the nineteenth century.

AN UNEXPECTED KINSHIP

As humanism in its development was becoming more and more materialistic, it also increasingly allowed its concepts to be used first by socialism and then by communism. So that Karl Marx was able to say, in 1844, that "communism is naturalized humanism."

This statement has proved to be not entirely unreasonable. One does see the same stones in the foundations of an eroded humanism and of any type of socialism: boundless materialism; freedom from religion and religious responsibility (which under Communist regimes attains the form of antireligious dictatorship); concentration on social structures with an allegedly scientific approach. (This last is typical of both the Age of Enlightenment and Marxism.) It is no accident that all of communism's rhetorical vows revolve around Man (with a capital *M*) and his earthly happiness. At first glance this seems a grotesque comparison: common traits in the thinking and way of life of today's West and today's East? But such is the logic in the development of materialism.

The interrelationship is such, moreover, that

the current of materialism which is farthest to the left, and is hence the most consistent, always proves to be stronger, more attractive, and victorious. Humanism which has lost its Christian heritage cannot prevail in this competition. Thus during the past centuries and especially in recent decades, as the process became more acute, the alignment of forces was as follows: Liberalism was inevitably pushed aside by radicalism, radicalism had to surrender to socialism, and socialism could not stand up to communism. The Communist regime in the East could endure and grow due to the enthusiastic support from an enormous number of Western intellectuals who (feeling the kinship!) refused to see communism's crimes, and when they no longer could do so, they tried to justify these crimes. The problem persists: In our Eastern countries, communism has suffered a complete ideological defeat; it is zero and less than zero. And yet Western intellectuals still look at it with considerable interest and empathy, and this is precisely what makes it so immensely difficult for the West to withstand the East.

BEFORE THE TURN

I am not examining the case of a disaster brought on by a world war and the changes which it would produce in society. But as long as we wake up every morning under a peaceful sun, we must lead an everyday life. Yet there is a disaster which is already very much with us. I am referring to the calamity of an autonomous, irreligious humanistic consciousness.

It has made man the measure of all things on earth—imperfect man, who is never free of pride, self-interest, envy, vanity, and dozens of other defects. We are now paying for the mistakes which were not properly appraised at the beginning of the journey. On the way from the Renaissance to our days we have enriched our experience, but we have lost the concept of a Supreme Complete Entity which used to restrain our passions and our irresponsibility. We have placed too much hope in politics and social reforms, only to find out that we were being deprived of our most precious possession: our spiritual life. It is trampled by Party hucksters in the East, by commercial ones in the West. This is the essence of the crisis: the split in the world is less terrifying than the similarity of the disease afflicting its main sections.

If, as claimed by humanism, man were born only to be happy, he would not be born to die. Since his body is doomed to death, his task on earth evidently must be more spiritual: not a total engrossment in everyday life, not the search for the best ways to obtain material goods and then their carefree consumption. It has to be the fulfillment of a permanent, earnest duty so that one's life journey may become above all an experience of moral growth: to leave life a better human being than one started it. It is imperative to reappraise the scale of the usual human values; its present incorrectness is astounding. It is not possible that assessment of the President's performance should be reduced to the question of how much money one makes or to the availability of gasoline. Only by the voluntary nurturing in ourselves of freely accepted and serene self-restraint can mankind rise above the world stream of materialism.

Today it would be retrogressive to hold on to the ossified formulas of the Enlightenment. Such social dogmatism leaves us helpless before the trials of our times.

Even if we are spared destruction by war, life will have to change in order not to perish on its own. We cannot avoid reassessing the fundamental definitions of human life and human society. Is it true that man is above everything? Is there no Superior Spirit above him? Is it right that man's life and society's activities should be ruled by material expansion above all? Is it permissible to promote such expansion to the detriment of our integral spiritual life?

If the world has not approached its end, it has reached a major watershed in history, equal in importance to the turn from the Middle Ages to the Renaissance. It will demand from us a spiritual effort; we shall have to rise to a new height of vision, to a new level of life, where our physical nature will not be cursed, as in the Middle Ages, but even more importantly, our spiritual being will not be trampled upon, as in the Modern Era.

This ascension is similar to climbing onto the next anthropological stage. No one on earth has any other way left but—upward.

LETTER TO THE SOVIET LEADERS

*Translated from the Russian
by Hilary Sternberg*

PREFACE

Written some time before the seizure of The Gulag Archipelago *by the KGB, my letter with all these proposals was mailed to its destination almost six months ago. Since then there has been no answer, no reaction of any kind, nor any movement toward one. The closed deliberations of our governmental apparatus have of course doomed many ideas of more obvious import than this. There remains nothing further I can do now except make the letter public. The press campaign against* Gulag *and the refusal to acknowledge the irrefutable past might have been considered a final rejection. But even today I cannot consider this irreversible. It is never too late for repentance; this path is open to every living human being, to everyone capable of life.*

This letter owes its conception and development to a single concern: how to avoid the national ca-

tastrophe that threatens our land. Certain of its specific proposals may seem surprising, but I am ready to withdraw them at once, were someone to offer criticism which is not a facile play of wit but a constructive alternative route, a better way out, one that is above all fully realizable, with clear lines of approach. Our intelligentsia is unanimous in its conception of what would constitute a desirable future for our country (the most sweeping kinds of liberties), but it is equally unanimous in its lack of exertion toward achieving this aim. They wait as though bewitched, wondering whether something might not happen of its own accord. Well, it won't.

In advancing my proposals, I of course had very little hope, and yet was not without any hope whatever. The fact of the "Khrushchev miracle" of 1955–1956 is ground enough for such faith: the unforeseen and unbelievable miracle of releasing millions of innocent prisoners, linked as it was with the rudiments—soon broken off—of humane legislation. (Yet in other fields and at the very same time, the other hand was amassing items with the contrary significance.) This flurry of activity on Khrushchev's part went far beyond any political maneuver he might have needed, and was undoubtedly sincere; in its essence it was an act hostile to and incompatible with communist ideology (which explains the hurry to repudiate his actions and the methodical arm's-length attitude toward him). To forbid the supposition that something of this sort could ever recur would mean to slam the door on any hope for a peaceful evolution of our country.

A.S.

January 1974

INTRODUCTION

I do not entertain much hope that you will deign to examine ideas not formally solicited by you, although they come from a fellow countryman of a rare kind—one who does not stand on a ladder subordinate to your command, who can be neither dismissed from his post, nor demoted, nor promoted, nor rewarded by you, and from whom therefore you are almost certain to hear an opinion sincerely voiced, without any careerist calculations, such as you are unlikely to hear from even the finest experts in your bureaucracy. I do not hold out much hope, but I shall try to say what is most important in a short space—namely, to set forth what I hold to be for the good and salvation of our people, to which all of you—and I myself— belong.

That was no slip of the tongue. I wish all people well, and the closer they are to us and the more dependent upon us, the more fervent is my wish. But it is the fate of the Russian and Ukrainian peoples that preoccupies me above all, for, as the proverb says: It's where you're born that you can be most useful. And there is a deeper reason too: the incomparable sufferings of our people.

I am writing this letter on the *supposition* that you, too, are swayed by this primary concern, that you are not alien to your origins, to your fathers, grandfathers, and great-grandfathers, to the expanses of your homeland; that you have not lost all feeling of nationality. If I am mistaken, there is no point in your reading the rest of this letter.

I am not about to plunge into the harrowing details of the last sixty years. I try to explain the course of our history, and what sort of history it has been, in my books, which I doubt that you have read or will ever read. But it is to you in particular that I address this letter, in order to set forth my view of the future, which seems to me correct, and perhaps even to convince you. And to suggest to you, while there is still time, a possible way out of the chief dangers facing our country in the next ten to thirty years.

These dangers are: war with China; and our destruction, together with Western civilization, in the crush and stench of a befouled earth.

THE WEST ON ITS KNEES

Neither after the Crimean War, nor, more recently, after the war with Japan, nor in 1916, 1921, 1931, or 1941, would even the most unbridled patriotic soothsayer have dared to set forth so arrogant a prospect: that the time was approaching, indeed was close at hand, when all the great European powers taken together would cease to exist as a serious physical force; that their rulers would resort to all manner of concessions simply to win the favor of the rulers of a future Russia, would even vie with one another to gain that favor, just so long as the Russian press would stop abusing them; and that they would grow so weak, without losing a single war; that countries proclaiming themselves "neutral" would seek every opportunity to gratify us and pander to us; that our eternal dream of controlling *straits,* although never realized, would be made irrelevant by the giant strides that Russia took into the Mediterranean and the oceans; that only fear of economic losses and extra administrative chores would become the arguments against Russian expansion to the West; and that even the mightiest transatlantic power, having emerged all-victorious from two world wars as the leader and provider for all mankind, would suddenly lose to a tiny, distant Asiatic country, and show internal dissension and spiritual weakness.

Truly the foreign policy of Tsarist Russia never had any successes to compare with these. Even after she had won the great European war against Napoleon, she did not extend her power over Eastern Europe in any way. She undertook to crush the Hungarian revolution—to help the Hapsburgs. She covered the Prussian rear in 1866 and 1870 without gaining anything in exchange— that is, she disinterestedly advanced the power of the German states. They, on the other hand, entangled her in a series of Balkan and Turkish wars, where she lost repeatedly, and despite her enormous resources and vast designs, she never did succeed in realizing the dreams of her leading circles to acquire the straits, although she entered her last (and for herself fatal) war with precisely this as her chief aim. Tsarist Russia often found herself carrying out other people's missions quite unconnected with her own. Many of her foreign policy blunders were the result of a lack of practical calculation at the top and a cumbersome, bureaucratic diplomatic service, but they also seem at times to have been connected with a certain streak of idealism in the thinking of her rulers, which hindered them from taking a consistent line in defense of the national self-interest.

Soviet diplomacy has rid itself of all these weaknesses, root and branch. It knows how to make demands, exact concessions, simply get things, in ways that Tsarism never knew. In terms of its actual achievements it might even be regarded as brilliant; in fifty years, with only one large-scale war, which it won from a position no whit more advantageous than that of the other participants, it rose from a country riven by civil strife to a superpower before which the entire world trembles. There have been some particularly striking moments when success was piled on success. For instance, at the end of the Second World War, when Stalin, who had always easily outmaneuvered Roosevelt, outmaneuvered Churchill too and not only got all he wanted in Europe and Asia, but also got back with ease (probably to his own surprise) the hundreds of thousands of Soviet citizens in Austria and Italy who were determined not to return home but who were betrayed by the Western Allies through a combination of deceit and force. No less an achievement than Stalin's have been the successes of Soviet diplomacy in recent years: for the Western world, as a single, clearly united force, no longer counterbalances the Soviet Union, indeed has almost ceased to exist. In finding the unity, steadfastness, and courage to face the Second World War, and then the reserves of strength to pull itself out of postwar ruin, Europe appears to have exhausted itself for a long time to come. For no external reasons, the victorious powers have grown weak and effete.

At the peak of such staggering successes, the last thing a person wants to hear is other people's opinions and doubts. This, of course, is the worst possible time I could have chosen to approach you with advice or exhortations. For when outward successes come thick and fast, it is the hardest thing in the world to desist from piling up more, to place limitations on oneself and to change one's whole outlook.

But this is where the wise differ from the unwise: they heed advice and counsels of caution long before the need becomes overwhelming.

Furthermore, there is much about these successes that gives little cause for self-congratulation. The catastrophic weakening of the Western world and the whole of Western civilization is by no means due solely to the success of a relentless, single-minded Soviet foreign policy. It is, rather, the result of a historical, psychological, and moral crisis affecting the totality of culture and the view of the world which arose at the time of the Renaissance and attained its highest expression with the eighteenth-century Enlightenment. An analysis of that crisis is beyond the scope of this letter.

And something else one notices—and cannot fail to notice—about our successes is two astonishing failures: amid our accomplishments *we ourselves raised* two ferocious enemies for Russia, one for the last war and the other for the next war—the German Wehrmacht and Mao Tse-tung's China. Circumventing the Treaty of Versailles, we helped the German Wehrmacht train their first officers on Soviet training grounds, where they

received their first experience of the theory of
modern warfare, tank thrusts, and airborne land-
ings, all of which later proved very useful to Hitler's army with its limited time for military prepa-
rations. And the story of how we bred Mao
Tse-tung in place of a peaceable neighbor such as
Chiang Kai-shek, and helped him in the atomic
race, is closer in time and better known. (Are we
not heading for a similar failure with the Arabs
also?)

And here we come to the crux of the matter we
are discussing: These failures stemmed not from
mistakes committed by our diplomats, nor from
the miscalculations of our generals, but from an
*exact adherence to the precepts of Marxism-Lenin-
ism*—i.e., in the first instance, to harm the cause
of world imperialism, and in the second, to support Communist movements abroad. In both cases
national considerations were completely lacking.

I am well aware that I am talking to total realists
and I shall not waste my breath on appeals such as:
Oh, if only we could retrieve just a little of the
bumbling idealism of the old Russian diplomacy!
Or: Let's do the world a favor and keep our nose
out of its business. Or: Let's take a closer look at
the moral foundations of our victorious foreign

policy—it brings the Soviet Union power abroad, but does it bring any real benefit to her peoples?

I am talking to total realists, and the simplest thing is to name the danger of which you have a much more detailed knowledge than I, for you have already been looking uneasily in its direction (and rightly so) for a long time: *China.*

As our proverb has it: As the forest grew, so the ax handle grew with it.

However much you may triumph today and however high you may rise in your own estimation, yet one must always be reminded that in the history of the world there has never been (and will never be) a force for which there would exist no counterforce.

In this case, nine hundred million ax handles.

WAR WITH CHINA

I hope you will not repeat the mistakes made by many of the world's rulers before you: don't reckon on any triumphant blitzkrieg. You will have against you a country of almost a *thousand million* people, the like of which has never yet gone to war in the history of the world. The time

since 1949 has evidently not been enough for the
population to lose its high degree of traditional
industriousness (which is higher than ours is
today), its tenacity and submissiveness; and it is
firmly in the grip of a totalitarian system no whit
more tractable than ours. Its army and population
will not surrender en masse with Western good
sense, when it is neither surrounded nor beaten.
Every soldier and every civilian will fight to the
last bullet, the last breath. We shall have no ally in
that war, none at least the size of, say, India. You
will not, of course, be the first to use nuclear weapons; that would do irreparable damage to your
reputation, which you cannot disregard, and from
a practical point of view wouldn't bring you a
quick victory anyway. The opposing side, being
more poorly equipped in this respect, is even less
likely to use them. (And in general, fortunately,
mankind has been able to hold itself back from the
ultimate brink of destruction by virtue of its simple instinct for self-preservation. Thus it was that
after the First World War no one dared to use
chemical warfare, and thus it is, I believe, that now
after the Second no one will use nuclear weapons.
So all the ruinously extravagant superstockpiling
that is going on is senseless and gratifies only the

scientists and the generals—this is the hard fate of those countries who have elected to be in the front ranks of the nuclear powers. The stockpiled weapons will never be of any use; and by the time the conflict erupts they will also be obsolete.)

A *conventional* war, on the other hand, would be the longest and bloodiest of all the wars mankind has ever fought. Like the Vietnam War at the very least (to which it will be similar in many ways), it will certainly last a minimum of ten to fifteen years—and, incidentally, will run almost exactly along the lines forecast by Amalrik, who was sent to his destruction for what he wrote instead of being invited to join the inner circle of our advisers. If Russia lost up to one and a half million people in the First World War and (according to Khrushchev's figures) twenty million in the Second, then war with China is bound to cost us sixty million souls at the very least, and, as always in wars, they will be the best souls—all our finest and purest people are bound to perish. As for the Russian people, our very last root will be extirpated. And this will be the climax of a long line of extirpations, beginning in the seventeenth century with the extermination of the Old Believers, continuing with Peter the Great and a string of successors (which I will also leave to one side in this letter), and ending with this, the ultimate one. After *this* war the Russian people will virtually cease to exist on this planet. And that alone will mean the war has been lost *utterly,* irrespective of all its other consequences (for the most part dismal, including the consequences for your power, as you realize). One's heart bleeds at the thought of our young men and all the best part of our middle generation, marching and riding off to die in a war. To die in an *ideological* war! And mainly for a dead ideology! I think *even you* are not able to take such a terrible responsibility upon yourselves!

One aches with sympathy for the ordinary Chinese too, because it is they who will be the most helpless victims of the war. They are held in such a strait jacket that not only can they not change their fate or discuss it in any way, they daren't even wiggle their ears!

This calamitous future, which is just around the corner at the current rate of development, weighs heavily on us creatures of the present—on those who wield power, on those who have the power of influence, and on those who have only a voice to cry: There must never be such a war. *This war must not happen, ever!* Our task must be not to *win* the war, for no one can possibly win it, but to *avoid* it!

I think I can see a way. And that is why I have undertaken to write this letter today.

Why are we veering toward this war? For two reasons. One is the dynamic pressure of a China one thousand million strong on our as yet unexploited Siberian lands—not the strip that is now being disputed on the basis of past treaties, but the whole of Siberia—to which, in our scramble for great social and even cosmic transformations, we haven't yet bent our energies. And this pressure will increase as the earth becomes increasingly overpopulated. But the main reason for this impending war, a reason that is far more powerful and indeed is the chief and insuperable one, is *ideological.* This should not surprise us: throughout history there have been no crueler wars and periods of civil strife than those provoked by ideological (including, alas, religious) dissensions. For fifteen years now a dispute has been going on between yourselves and the Chinese leaders over which of you best understands, expounds, and propagates the doctrines of the Fathers of the Progressive World View. And in addition to a fierce power struggle, there is this global rivalry devel-

oping between you, this claim to be the sole true
exponent of Communist doctrine and this ambi-
tion to be the one to lead all the peoples of the
world after you in carrying it out.

And what do you think will happen? That when
war breaks out, both the belligerents will simply
fly the purity of their ideology on their flags? And
that sixty million of our fellow countrymen will
allow themselves to be killed because the sacred
truth is written on page 533 of Lenin and not on
page 335, as our adversary claims? Surely only the
very, very first of them will die for that. . . .

When war with Hitler began, Stalin, who had
omitted and bungled so much in the way of military preparation, did not neglect *that* side, the
ideological side. And although the ideological
grounds for that war seemed more indisputable
than those that face you now (the war was waged
against what appeared on the surface to be a diametrically opposed ideology), from the very first
days of the war Stalin refused to rely on the moldy,
decaying prop of ideology. He wisely discarded it,
all but ceased to mention it, and unfurled instead
the old Russian banner and to a certain extent
even the standard of Russian Orthodoxy—and we
conquered! (Only toward the end of the war and

after the victory was the Progressive Doctrine once again hauled out of its mothballs.)

So do you really think that in a conflict between similar, closely related ideologies, differing only in nuances, *you* will not have to make the same re-orientation? But by then it will be too late—military tension alone will make it very difficult.

How much wiser it would be to make *this same* turnabout today as a preventive measure. If it has to be done anyway *for a war,* wouldn't it be more sensible to do it much earlier, *to avoid going to war at all?*

Give them their ideology! Let the Chinese leaders glory in it for a while. And for that matter, let them shoulder the whole sackful of unfulfillable international obligations, let them grunt and heave and instruct humanity, and foot all the bills for their absurd economics (a million a day just to Cuba), and let them support terrorists and guerrillas in the southern hemisphere too, if they like.

The main source of the savage feuding between us will then melt away, a great many points of today's contention and conflict all over the world will also melt away, and a military clash will become a much remoter possibility and perhaps *won't take place at all.*

Take an unbiased look: the murky whirlwind of *Progressive Ideology* swept in on us from the West at the end of the last century, and has tormented and ravaged our soul quite enough; and if it is now veering away farther east of its own accord, then let it veer away, don't try to stop it! (This doesn't mean I wish for the spiritual destruction of China. I believe that our people will soon be cured of this disease, and the Chinese too, given time; and it will not be too late, I hope, to save their country and protect humanity. But after all we have endured, it is enough for the time being for us to worry about how to save *our own* people.)

Ideological dissension will melt away—and there will probably never be a Sino-Soviet war. And if there should be, then it will be in the remote future and a truly defensive, truly patriotic one. At the end of the twentieth century we cannot give up Siberian territory; that's beyond all question. But to give up an ideology can only mean relief and recovery for us!

CIVILIZATION IN AN IMPASSE

A second danger is the multiple impasse in which Western civilization (which Russia long ago chose the honor of joining) finds itself, but it is not so imminent; there are still two or three decades in reserve. We share this impasse with all the advanced countries, which are in an even worse and more perilous predicament than we are, although people keep hoping for new scientific loopholes and inventions to stave off the day of retribution. I would not mention this danger in this letter if the solutions to both problems were not identical in many respects, if one and the same turnabout, a *single* decision, would not deliver us from *both* dangers. Such a happy coincidence is rare. Let us value history's gift and not miss these opportunities.

And all this has so "suddenly" come tumbling out at mankind's feet, and at Russia's! How fond our progressive essayists were, both before and after the Revolution, of ridiculing those *retrogrades* (there were always so many of them in Russia) who called upon us to spare our past and to cherish it, even the most Godforsaken hamlet with a couple of hovels, even on the paths that run alongside the railway track; who called upon us to keep horses even after the advent of the motorcar, not to abandon small factories for enormous plants and industrial complexes, not to discard organic manure in favor of chemical fertilizers, not to mass by the million in cities, not to clamber on top of one another in multistory apartment blocks. How they laughed, how they tormented those reactionary "Slavophiles" (the gibe became the accepted term; the simpletons never managed to think up another name for themselves). They hounded the men who said that it was perfectly feasible for a colossus like Russia, with all its spiritual peculiarities and folk traditions, to find its own particular path; and that it could not be that the whole of mankind should follow a single, absolutely identical pattern of development.

No, we had to be dragged along the whole of the Western bourgeois-industrial and Marxist path in order to discover, toward the close of the twentieth century, and again from progressive Western scholars, what any village graybeard in the Ukraine or Russia had understood from time immemorial and could have explained to the progressive commentators ages ago, had the commentators ever found the time in that dizzy fever of theirs to consult him: that a dozen worms can't go on and on gnawing the same apple *forever;* that if the earth is a *finite* object, then its expanses and resources are finite also, and the *endless, infinite* progress dinned into our heads by the dreamers of the Enlightenment cannot be accomplished on it. No, we had to shuffle on and on behind other people, without knowing what lay ahead of us, until suddenly we now hear the scouts calling to one another: We've blundered into a dead-end street, we'll have to turn back. All that "endless progress" turned out to be an insane, ill-considered, furious dash into a blind alley. A civilization greedy for "perpetual progress" has choked and is nearing its end.

And it is not "convergence" that faces us and the Western world now, but total renewal and reconstruction in both East and West, for both are in the same impasse. All this has been widely publicized and explained in the West thanks to the efforts of the Teilhard de Chardin Society and the Club of Rome. Here, in a very condensed form, are their conclusions.

Society must cease to look upon "progress" as something desirable. "Eternal progress" is a nonsensical myth. What must be implemented is not a "steadily expanding economy," but a *zero-growth economy,* a stable economy. *Economic growth is not only unnecessary but ruinous.* We must set ourselves the aim not of *increasing* national resources, but merely of *conserving* them. We must renounce, as a matter of urgency, the contemporary gigantism syndrome—in industry, in agriculture, and in urban development (the cities of today are cancerous tumors). The chief aim of technology will now be to eradicate the lamentable results of previous technologies. The "Third World," which has not yet started on the fatal path of Western civilization, can only be saved by "small-scale technology," which requires an increase, not a reduction, in manual labor, uses the simplest of machinery, and is based purely on local materials.

The most unrestrained industrial growth has taken place not over thousands or hundreds of years ("from Adam to 1945"), but only over the last twenty-eight years (from 1945 onward). It is this rapidity of growth in recent years that is most dangerous for mankind. The groups of scientists I mentioned have done computer studies based on various possible courses of economic development, and *all* these courses turned out to be *hopeless* and pointed ominously to the catastrophic destruction of mankind sometime between the years 2020 and 2070 *if it did not relinquish economic progress.* These calculations took into consideration five main factors: population, natural resources, agricultural production, industry, and environmental pollution. If the available information is to be believed, some of the earth's resources are rapidly running out: there will be no more oil in twenty years, no more copper in nineteen, no more mercury in twelve; many other resources are nearly exhausted; both energy and fresh water are very limited. But even if future exploration uncovers reserves twice or even three times as big as those we now know about, and even if agricultural output *doubles* and man succeeds in harnessing unlimited nuclear energy, *in all cases the population will be overtaken by mass destruction in the first decades of the twenty-first century*—if not because of production grinding to a halt (end of resources), then because of a production surplus (destruction of the environment)—and this whatever course we take.

When everything is staked on "progress," as it is now, it is *impossible* to find a *joint* optimum solution to *all five* of the problems referred to above. Unless mankind renounces the notion of economic progress, the biosphere will become unfit for life even *during our lifetime.* And if mankind is to be *saved,* technology has to be adapted to a stable economy in the next twenty to thirty years, and to do that, the process must be started *now, immediately.*

Actually, though, it is more than likely that Western civilization will not perish. It is so dynamic and so inventive that it will ride out even this impending crisis, will dismantle all its age-old misconceptions and in a few years set about the necessary reconstruction. And the "Third World" will heed the warnings in good time and *not take the Western path at all.* This is still perfectly feasible for most of the African and many of the Asian countries (and nobody will sneer at them and call them "Negrophiles").

But what about *us?* Us, with our unwieldiness and our inertia, with our flinching and our inability to change even a single letter, a single syllable, of what Marx said in 1848 about industrial development? Economically and physically we are perfectly capable of saving ourselves. But there is a roadblock on the path to our salvation—the sole

Progressive World View. If we renounce industrial development, what about the working class, socialism, communism, unlimited increase in productivity, and all the rest? Marx is not to be corrected; that's revisionism. . . .

But you are already being called "revisionists" anyway, whatever you may do in the future. So wouldn't it be better to do your duty soberly, responsibly, and firmly, and give up the dead letter for the sake of a living people who are utterly dependent on your power and your decisions? And you must do it without delay. Why dawdle if we shall have to snap out of it sometime anyway? Why repeat what others have done and loop the agonizing loop right to the end, when we are not too far into it to turn back? If the man at the head of the column cries, "I have lost my way," do we absolutely have to plow right on to the spot where he realized his mistake and only there turn back? Why not turn and start on the right course from wherever we happen to be?

As it is, we have followed Western technology too long and too faithfully. We are supposed to be the "first socialist country in the world," one which sets an example to other peoples, in both the East and the West, and we are supposed to have been so "original" in following various monstrous doctrines—on the peasantry, on small tradesmen—so why, then, have we been so depressingly unoriginal in technology, and why have we so unthinkingly, so blindly, copied Western civilization? (Why? From military haste, of course, and the haste stems from our immense "international responsibilities," and all this because of Marxism again.)

One might have thought that with the central planning of which we are so proud, we of all people had the chance *not* to spoil Russia's natural beauty, *not* to create antihuman, multimillion concentrations of people. But we've done everything the other way round: we have dirtied and defiled the wide Russian spaces and disfigured the heart of Russia, our beloved Moscow. What crazed, unfilial hand bulldozed the boulevards so that you can't go along them now without diving down into degrading tunnels of stone? What evil, alien ax broke up the tree-lined boulevards of the Sadovoye Koltso and replaced them with a poisoned zone of asphalt and gasoline? The irreplaceable face of the city and all the ancient city plan have been obliterated, and imitations of the West are being flung up, like the New Arbat; the city has been so squeezed, stretched, and pushed upward that life has become intolerable—so what do we do now? Reconstruct the former Moscow in a new place? That seems to be impossible. Accept, then, that we have lost it completely?

We have squandered our resources foolishly without so much as a backward glance, sapped our soil, mutilated our vast expanses with idiotic "inland seas," and contaminated belts of wasteland around our industrial centers—but for the moment, at least, far more still remains untainted by us, which we haven't had time to touch. So let us come to our senses in time, let us change our course!

THE RUSSIAN NORTHEAST

And here there is some extra hope for us, for there is one peculiarity, one reservation, in the arguments of the scientists I mentioned earlier. That reservation is: *The supreme asset* of all peoples is now *the earth.* The earth as open space for settling. The earth as the totality of the biosphere. The earth as a cloak over our deeply buried resources. The earth as fertile soil. Nevertheless, the prognoses for fertility are gloomy too: land resources averaged out over the planet as a whole, including any rise in fertility, will be exhausted by the year 2000, and if agricultural output can be *doubled* (not by the collective farms, of course, not by us), fertility, *on average for the planet as a whole,* will still be exhausted by 2030. But there are four fortunate countries still abundantly rich in untapped land even today. They are: Russia (that is not a slip of the tongue: it is precisely the RSFSR that I mean), Australia, Canada, and Brazil.

And herein lies Russia's hope for winning time and winning salvation: In our vast northeastern spaces, which over four centuries our sluggishness has prevented us from mutilating by our mistakes, we can build *anew:* not the senseless, voracious civilization of "progress"—no; we can set up a *stable* economy without pain or delay and settle people there for the first time according to the needs and principles of that economy. These spaces allow us to hope that Russia will not perish in the general crisis of Western civilization. (And there are many lands even nearer at hand, lands that have been abandoned through collective-farm neglect.)

Let us, without any dogmatic preconceptions,

recall Stolypin and give him his due. Speaking in the state Duma in 1908 he asserted prophetically: *"The land is a guarantee of our strength in the future, the land is Russia."* And on the subject of the Amur railroad he said: "If we remain plunged in our lethargic sleep, these lands will be running with foreign sap, and when we wake up they will perhaps be Russian in name only."

Today, because of the confrontation with China, this danger is spreading until it threatens virtually the whole of our Siberia. Two dangers merge, but by a stroke of good fortune, a single way out of both of them presents itself: *reject the dead ideology* that threatens to destroy us militarily and economically, throw away all its fantastic alien global missions, and concentrate on opening up (on the principles of a stable, nonprogressive economy) the Russian Northeast—the Northeast of European Russia and the North of the Asian part, together with the main Siberian massif.

We shall not nurture hopes—we shall not hasten the cataclysm which is perhaps ripening, perhaps will even come to pass in the Western countries. These hopes may be deceived, just as the hopes for China were in the 1940s: if new social systems are created in the West, they may prove even harsher and more unfriendly to us than the present ones. And let's leave the Arabs to their fate; they have Islam, they'll sort themselves out. And let's leave South America to itself; nobody is threatening to take it over. And let's leave Africa to find out for itself how to start on an independent road to statehood and civilization, and simply wish it the good fortune not to repeat the mistakes of "uninterrupted progress." For half a century we have busied ourselves with world revolution, extending our influence over Eastern Europe and over other continents; with the reform of agriculture according to ideological principles; with the annihilation of the landowning classes; with the eradication of Christian religion and morality; with the showy but useless space race; of course with arming ourselves and others whenever they want it; with everything and anything, in fact, but developing and tending our country's chief asset, the Northeast. Our people are not going to live in space, or in Southeast Asia, or in Latin America: it is Siberia and the North that are our hope and our reservoir.

It may be said that even there we have *done* a lot, built a great deal, but we have done less of building than of destroying people, as it was with the "death road" from Salekhard to Igarka (but let's not go through all those prison camp stories here). Building the railroad around Lake Baikal so that it became flooded, and sending the loop line senselessly through the mountains, so that the brakes burned, building things like the pulp mills on Lake Baikal and the Selenga River, the quicker to profit and poison—we would have done better to wait awhile. In terms of the speed of development in this century we have done very little in the Northeast. But today we can say: How fortunate that it *is* so little, for now we can do everything rationally, right from the start, according to the principles of a stable economy. Today that "little" is still fortunate; but in a very short time it will already be a disaster.

And what irony: for half a century, since 1920, we have proudly (and rightly) refused to entrust the exploitation of our natural resources to foreigners—this may have looked like budding national aspirations. But we went on and on dragging our feet and wasting more and more time. And suddenly now, when it has been revealed that the world's energy resources are drying up, we, a great industrial superpower, like the meanest of backward countries, invite foreigners to exploit our mineral wealth and, by way of payment, suggest that they carry off our priceless treasure, Siberian natural gas—for which our children will curse us in half a generation's time as irresponsible prodigals. (We would have had plenty of other fine goods to barter if our industry had not also been built chiefly on . . . *ideology*. Once again ideology stands in the way of our people!)

I would not consider it moral to recommend a policy of saving only ourselves, when the difficulties are universal, had our people not suffered more in the twentieth century, as I believe they have, than any other people in the world. *In addition to* the toll of two world wars, we have lost, as a result of civil strife and tumult alone—as a result of internal political and economic "class" extermination alone—66 (sixty-six) million people!!! That is the calculation of a former Leningrad professor of statistics, I. A. Kurganov, and you can have it brought to you whenever you wish. I am no trained statistician, I cannot undertake to verify it; and anyway all statistics are kept secret in our country, and this is an indirect calculation. But it's true: a hundred million *are no more* (exactly *a hundred*, just as Dostoyevsky prophesied!), and with and without wars we have lost *one third* of the population we could now have had and almost *half* of the one we in fact have! What other people has had to pay such a price? After *such* losses, we may permit ourselves a little luxury, the way an invalid is given a rest after a serious illness. We need to heal our wounds, cure our national body and natural spirit. Let us find the strength, sense, and courage to put our own house in order before we busy ourselves with the cares of the entire planet.

And once again, by a happy coincidence, the whole world can only gain by it.

Another moral objection may be raised: that our Northeast is not entirely Russia's, that a historical sin was committed in conquering it; large numbers of the local inhabitants were wiped out (but nothing to compare with our own recent self-extermination) and others were harried. Yes, it was so, it happened in the sixteenth century, but there is nothing whatsoever we can do now to rectify *that.* Since then, these spreading expanses have remained almost unpeopled, or even entirely so. According to the census, the people of the North number 128,000 in all, thinly scattered and strung out across vast distances. We would not be crowding them in the slightest by opening up the North. Quite the contrary, we are now sustaining their way of life and their existence as a matter of course; they seek no separate destiny for themselves and would be unable to find one. Of all the ethnic problems facing our country, this is the least; it hardly exists.

And so there is one way out for us (and the sooner we take it, the more effective it will be), namely, for the state to switch its attention away from distant continents—and even away from Europe and the south of our country—and make the Northeast the center of national activity and settlement and a focus for the aspirations of young people.*

INTERNAL, NOT EXTERNAL, DEVELOPMENT

This switching of the focus of our attention and efforts will need to take place, of course, in more than just the geographical sense: not only from external to internal land masses, but also from external to internal problems—in all senses, from outer to inner. The actual—not the ostensible—

*Of course, a switch of this kind would oblige us sooner or later to withdraw our protective surveillance of Eastern Europe. Nor can there be any question of any peripheral nation being forcibly kept within the bounds of our country.

condition of our people, our families, our schools, our nation, our spirit, our life style, and our economy demands this of you.

Let us begin at the end, with agriculture. It is a paradox, impossible to believe: that such a great power, one of such military might and with such brilliant foreign policy successes, should be in such an impasse, and in such desperate straits with its economy. Everything we have achieved here has been gained not by brains but by numbers, that is, through the extravagant expenditure of human energies and material. Everything we create costs us far more than it is worth, but the state allows itself to disregard the expense. Our "ideological agriculture" has already become the laughing-stock of the entire world, and with the worldwide shortage of foodstuffs, it will soon be a burden on it as well. Famine rages in many parts of the world, and will rage even more fiercely because of over-population, scarcity of land, and the problems of emergence from colonialism. In other words, people cannot produce the *grain*. We, who should be able to, however, don't produce enough, or we are shaken by one year of drought (and doesn't the history of farming tell us of cases of seven such years in succession?). And all because we *won't* admit our blunder over the collective farms. For centuries Russia *exported* grain—ten to twelve million tons a year just before the First World War —and here we are after fifty-five years of the new order and forty years of the much-vaunted collective farm system, forced to *import* twenty million tons per year! It's shameful—it really is time we came to our senses! The village, for centuries the mainstay of Russia, has become its chief weakness! For too many decades we have sapped the collectivized village of all its strength, driven it to utter despair, and now at last we have begun *giving back* its treasures and paying it fair prices—but *too late.* Its interest and faith in its work have been drained. As the old saying goes: Rebuff a man and riches won't buy him back. With the impending worldwide shortage of grain, there is only one way for us to fill the people's bellies: give up the forced collective farms and leave just the voluntary ones. And set up in the wide-open spaces of our Northeast (at great expense, admittedly) the kind of agricultural system that will produce foodstuffs at a natural economic tempo, and will not require waves of Party agitators and mobilized labor from the towns.

I assume you know (it's obvious from your decrees) about the state of affairs throughout our national economy and throughout our gargantuan civil service: people don't put any effort at all into their official duties and have no enthusiasm for them, but cheat (and sometimes steal) as much as they can and spend their office hours doing private jobs (they're forced to, with wages as low as they are today; for nobody is strong enough and no lifetime long enough to earn a living from official wages alone). Everybody is trying to make more money for less work. If this is the mood of the nation, what sort of time scale can we work to for saving the country?

But even more destructive is vodka. That's something else you know about, there was even that decree of yours—but did it change anything? So long as vodka is an important item of state revenue, nothing will change, and we shall simply go on ravaging the people's vitals for the sake of profit. (I worked in a consumers' cooperative when I was in exile, and I distinctly remember that vodka amounted to 60 to 70 percent of our turnover.)

Bearing in mind the state of people's morals, their spiritual condition, and their relations with one another and with society, all the *material* achievements we trumpet so proudly are petty and worthless.

When we set about what, in geographical terms, we shall call the opening up of the Northeast, and, in economic terms, the building of a stable econ- omy, and when we tackle all the technical prob- lems (construction, transportation, and social orga- nization), we must also recognize, inherent in all these aspects, the existence of a *moral* dimension. The physical and spiritual health of the people must be at the heart of the entire exercise, includ- ing every stage and part.

The construction of more than half our state in a fresh new place will enable us to avoid repeating the disastrous errors of the twentieth century with respect to industry, roads, and cities. If we are to stop sweating over the short-term economic needs of today and create a land of clean air and clean water for our children, we must renounce many forms of industrial production which result in toxic waste. Military obligations dictate, you say? But in fact we have only *one tenth* of the military obligations that we pretend to have, or rather that we intensively and assiduously create for ourselves by inventing interests in the Atlantic and Indian oceans. For the next half century our only genuine military need will be to defend ourselves against China, and it would be better not to go to war with her at all. A well-established Northeast is also our best defense against China. *No one else on earth* threatens us, and no one is going to attack us. For peacetime we are armed to excess several times over; we manufacture vast quantities of arms that we shall constantly have to exchange for new ones; and we are training far more manpower than we require, who will anyway be past the service age by the time the military need arises.

From all sides except China we have ample guarantees of security for a long time to come, which means that we can make drastic cuts in our military investment for many years ahead and throw the released resources into the economy and the reorganization of our life. For technological extinction is no less a threat than war.

The time has also come to exempt the youth of Russia from universal, compulsory military service, which exists neither in China, nor in the United States, nor in any other large country in the world. We maintain this army solely out of military and diplomatic vanity—for reasons of prestige and conceit; also for expansion abroad, which we must give up if we are to achieve our own physical and spiritual salvation; and finally in the misguided notion that the only way to *educate* young men to be of use to the state is to have them spend years going through the mill of army training. Even if it is ever acknowledged that we cannot secure our defense otherwise than by putting *everybody* through the army, the period of service could nevertheless be greatly reduced and army "education" humanized. Under the present system, we as people lose *inwardly* far more than we gain from all these parades.

In reducing our military force we shall also deliver our skies from the tiresome roar of aerial armadas—day and night, all the hours that God made, they perform their interminable flights and exercises over our broad lands, breaking the sound barrier, roaring and booming, shattering the daily life, rest, sleep, and nerves of hundreds of thousands of people, effectively addling their brains by screeching overhead (all the big bosses ban flights over their country estates); and all this has been going on for decades and has nothing at all to do with saving the country—it is a futile waste of energy. Give the country back a healthy *silence,* without which you cannot begin to have a healthy people.

The urban life, which, by now, as much as half our population is doomed to live, is utterly unnatural—and you agree entirely, every one of you, for every evening with one accord you all escape from the city to your dachas in the country. And you are all old enough to remember our old pre-automobile towns—towns made for people, horses, dogs— and streetcars too; towns which were humane, friendly, cozy places, where the air was always clean, which were snow-clad in winter and in spring redolent with garden smells streaming through the fences into the streets. There was a garden to almost every house and hardly a house more than two stories high—the pleasantest height for human habitation. The inhabitants of those towns were not nomads, they didn't have to decamp twice a year to save their children from a blazing inferno. An economy of *non* gigantism with small-scale though highly developed technology will not only allow for but necessitate the building of uncrowded cities congenial to man. And we can perfectly well set up road barriers at all the entrances and admit horses, and battery-powered electric vehicles, but not poisonous internal combustion engines, and if anybody has to dive underground at crossroads, let it be the vehicles, and not the old, the young, and the sick.

These are the sorts of towns that should adorn our frostbitten Northeast when it has been thawed out, and let those ill-spent funds applied to space research be poured into the thawing-out process instead.

It's true that there was another special feature of the old Russian towns, a spiritual one which made life there enjoyable even for the most highly educated and which meant they didn't have to conglomerate in a single capital city of seven million: many provincial towns—not just Irkutsk, Tomsk, Saratov, Yaroslavl, and Kazan, but many besides—were important cultural centers *in their own right.* But is it conceivable nowadays that we would allow any center of independent activity and thought to exist outside Moscow? Even Petersburg has quite lost its luster. There was a time when a unique and tremendously valuable book might be published in some little place like Vyshni Volochek—could our *ideology* conceivably allow that now? The present-day centralization of all forms of intellectual life is a monstrosity amounting to spiritual murder. Without these forty or eighty towns Russia does not exist as a country, but is merely some sort of inarticulate rump. So here again, at every step and in every direction, it is *ideology* that prevents us from building a healthy Russia.

A man's mental and emotional condition is inextricably linked with every aspect of his daily life. People who are forced to drive caterpillar tractors or massive-wheeled trucks down grassy byways and country lanes ill-suited and unprepared for them, churning up everything in their path, or who, out of greed, jolt a whole village awake at first light with the frenzied revving of a chain saw, become brutal and cynical. It is no accident either that there are these innumerable drunks and hooligans who pester women in the evenings and when they are not at work; if no police force can handle them, still less are they going to be restrained by an *ideology* that claims to be a substitute for morality. Having spent a fair amount of time working in both village and town schools, I can confidently state that our educational system is a poor teacher and a bad educator, and merely cheapens and squanders the childhood and hearts of our young people. Everything is so organized that the pupils have no reason at all to respect their teachers. Schooling will be genuine only when people of the highest caliber and with a real vocation go into teaching. But to achieve this we will have to expend untold energy and resources —and pay our teachers much better and make their position less humiliating. At the moment the teacher-training institute has the least prestige of almost all the institutes and grown men are ashamed to be schoolteachers. Secondary-school graduates flock to courses in military electronics like flies to a honey pot, but is it really for such sterile pursuits that we have been developing these last eleven hundred years?

Apart from not getting what they need from the schools, our future citizens don't get much from the family either. We are always boasting about our equality for women and our kindergartens, but we hide the fact that all this is just a substitute for the family we have undermined. Equality for women doesn't mean that they have to occupy *the same number* of factory jobs and office positions as men, but just that all these posts should in principle be equally open to women. In practice, a man's wage level ought to be such that whether he has a family of two or even four children, the woman *does not need* to earn a separate pay check and *does not need* to support her family financially on top of all her other toils and troubles. In pursuit of the Five-Year Plans and more manpower, we have never given our men the right sort of wages, with the result that the undermining and destruction of the family is part of the terrible price we have paid for those Five-Year Plans. How can one fail to feel shame and compassion at the sight of our women carrying heavy barrows of stones for paving the streets or for spreading on the tracks of our railway lines? When we contemplate such scenes, what more is there to say, what doubt can there possibly be? Who would hesitate to abandon the financing of South American revolutionaries in order to free our women from this bondage? Almost every sphere of activity is neglected and in desperate need of funds, hard work, and perseverance. Nor is *leisure* time an exception, reduced as it is to television, cards, dominoes, and that same old vodka; and if anybody *reads*, it is either sport or spy stories, or else that same old ideology in newspaper form. Can this really be that seductive socialism-cum-communism for which all those people laid down their lives, and for which sixty to ninety million perished?

The demands of *internal* growth are incomparably more important to us, as a people, than the need for any *external* expansion of our power. The whole of world history demonstrates that the peoples who created empires have always suffered spiritually as a result. The aims of a great empire and the moral health of the people are incompatible. We should not presume to invent international tasks and bear the cost of them so long as our people is in such moral disarray and we consider ourselves to be its sons.

And should we not also, perhaps, give up our Mediterranean aspirations while we are about it?

But to do that, we must first of all give up our ideology.

IDEOLOGY

This Ideology that fell to us by inheritance is not only decrepit and hopelessly antiquated now; even during its best decades it was totally mistaken in its predictions and was never a science.

A primitive, superficial economic theory, it declared that only the worker creates value and failed to take into account the contribution of either organizers, engineers, transportation, or marketing systems. It was mistaken when it forecast that the proletariat would be endlessly oppressed and would never achieve anything in a bourgeois democracy—if only we could shower people with as much food, clothing, and leisure as they have gained under capitalism! It missed the point when it asserted that the prosperity of the European countries depended on their colonies—it was only after they had shaken off the colonies that they began to accomplish their "economic miracles." It was mistaken through and through in its prediction that socialists could never come to power except through an armed uprising. It miscalculated in thinking that the first uprisings would take place in the advanced industrial countries—quite the reverse. And the picture of how the whole world would rapidly be overtaken by revolutions and how states would soon wither away was sheer delusion, sheer ignorance of human nature. And as for wars being characteristic of capitalism alone and coming to an end when capitalism did—we have already witnessed the longest war of the twentieth century so far, and it was not capitalism that rejected negotiations and a truce for fifteen to twenty years; and God forbid that we should witness the bloodiest and most brutal of all mankind's wars—a war between two Communist superpowers. Then there was nationalism, which this theory also buried in 1848 as a "survival"—but find a stronger force in the world today! And it's the same with many other things too tedious to list.

Marxism is not only not accurate, is not only not a science, has not only failed to predict a *single event* in terms of figures, quantities, time scales, or locations (something that electronic computers today do with laughable ease in the course of social forecasting, although never with the help of Marxism)—it absolutely astounds one by the economic and mechanistic crudity of its attempts to explain that most subtle of creatures, the human being, and that even more complex synthesis of millions of people, society. Only the cupidity of some, the blindness of others, and a craving for *faith* on the part of still others can serve to explain this grim jest of the twentieth century: how can such a discredited and bankrupt doctrine still have so many followers in the West! In *our* country are left the fewest of all! *We* who have had a taste of it are only pretending willy-nilly. . . .

We have seen above that it was not your common sense, but that same antiquated legacy of the Progressive Doctrine that endowed you with all the millstones that are dragging you down: the collectivization; then the nationalization of small trades and services (which has made the lives of ordinary citizens unbearable—but you don't feel that yourselves; which has caused thieving and lying to pile up and up even in the day-to-day running of the country—and you are powerless against it); then the need to inflate military development for the sake of making grand international gestures, so that the whole internal life of the country is going down the drain and in fifty-five years we haven't even found the time to open up Siberia; then the obstacles in the way of industrial development and technological reconstruction; then religious persecution, which is very important for Marxism,* but senseless and self-defeating for pragmatic state leaders—to set useless good-for-nothings to hounding the most conscientious workers, innocent of all cheating and theft, and as a result making everyone suffer from universal cheating and theft. For the believer his faith is *supremely* precious, more precious than the food he puts in his stomach. Have you ever paused to reflect on why it is that you deprive these millions

*Sergei Bulgakov demonstrated in *Karl Marx as a Religious Type* (1906) that atheism is the chief inspirational and emotional hub of Marxism and that all the rest of the doctrine has been added to this core. Ferocious hostility to religion is Marxism's most persistent feature.

of your finest subjects of their homeland? All this can do you as the leaders of the state nothing but harm, but you do it mechanically, automatically, because Marxism insists that you do it. Just as it insists that you, the rulers of a superpower, deliver accounts of your activities to visitors from distant parts—leaders of uninfluential, insignificant Communist parties from the other end of the globe, preoccupied least of all with the fortunes of Russia.

To someone brought up on Marxism it seems a terrifying step—suddenly to start living without the familiar Ideology. But in fact you have no choice, circumstances themselves will force you to do it, and it may already be too late. In anticipation of an impending war with China, Russia's national leaders will in any case have to rely on patriotism, and on patriotism alone. When Stalin initiated such a shift during the war—remember! —nobody was in the least surprised and nobody shed a tear for Marxism; everyone took it as the most natural thing in the world, something they recognized as Russian. It is only prudent to redeploy one's forces when faced by a great danger— but sooner rather than later. In any event, this process of repudiation, though tentative, began long ago in our country, for what is the "combination" of Marxism and patriotism but a meaningless absurdity? These two points of view can be "merged" only in generalized incantations, for history has shown us that in practice they are always diametrically opposed. This is so obvious that Lenin in 1915 actually proclaimed: "We are antipatriots." And that was the honest truth. And throughout the 1920s in our country the word "patriot" meant exactly the same as "White Guard." And the whole of this letter that I am now putting before you is patriotism, *which means* rejection of Marxism. For Marxism orders us to leave the Northeast unexploited and to leave our women with crowbars and shovels, and instead finance and expedite world revolution.

Beware when the first cannons fire on the Sino-Soviet border lest you find yourselves in a doubly precarious position because the national consciousness in our country has become stunted and blurred—witness how mighty America lost to tiny North Vietnam, how easily the nerves of American society and American youth gave way, precisely because the United States has a weak and undeveloped consciousness. Don't miss the chance while you've got it!

The step seems a hard one at first, but in fact,

once you have thrown off this pointless burden, you will quickly sense a huge relief and become aware of a relaxation in the entire structure of the state and in all the processes of government. After all, this Ideology, which is driving us into a situation of acute conflict abroad, has long ceased to be helpful to us here at home, as it was in the twenties and thirties. In our country today *nothing constructive rests upon it;* it is a sham theatrical prop made of plywood—take it away and nothing will collapse, nothing will even wobble. For a long time now, everything has rested solely on material calculation and the subjection of the people, and not on any upsurge of ideological enthusiasm, as you perfectly well know. This Ideology does nothing now but sap our strength and bind us. It clogs up the whole life of society—minds, tongues, radio, and press—with lies, lies, lies. For how else can something dead pretend that it is living except by erecting a scaffolding of lies? Everything is steeped in lies and *everybody knows it*—they say so openly in private conversation, joke about it, and are irked by it, but in their official speeches they go on hypocritically parroting what they are "supposed to say," and with equal hypocrisy and boredom read and listen to the speeches of others:

how much of society's energy is squandered on this! And you, when you open your newspapers or switch on your television—do *you yourselves* really believe for one instant that these speeches are sincere? No, you stopped believing long ago, I am certain of it. And if you didn't, then you must have become totally insulated from the inner life of the country.

This universal, obligatory force-feeding with lies is now the most agonizing aspect of existence in our country—worse than all our material miseries, worse than any lack of civil liberties.

All these arsenals of lies, which are totally unnecessary for our stability *as a state,* are levied as a kind of tax for the benefit of Ideology—to tie, strap events as they happen to a tenacious, sharp-clawed, but dead Ideology: and it is precisely because our state, through sheer force of habit, tradition, and inertia, continues to cling to this false doctrine with all its tortuous aberrations that it needs to put the dissenter behind bars. For a false *ideology* can find no other answer to argument and protest than weapons and prison bars.

Cast off this threadbare, flawed Ideology! Relinquish it to your rivals, let it go wherever it wants, let it pass from our country like a storm cloud, like an epidemic, let others concern themselves with it and study it, just as long as we don't! In ridding ourselves of it we shall also rid ourselves of the need to fill our lives with lies. Let us all pull off and shake off from all of us this filthy sweaty shirt of Ideology which is now so stained with the blood of those sixty-six million that it prevents the living body of the nation from breathing. This Ideology bears the entire responsibility for all the blood that has been shed. Do you need me to persuade you to throw it off without more ado? Whoever wants can pick it up in our place.

I am certainly not proposing that you go to the opposite extreme and persecute or ban Marxism, or even argue against it (nobody will argue against it for very long, if only out of sheer apathy). All I am suggesting is that you rescue yourselves from it, and rescue your state system and your people as well. *All you have to do* is to deprive Marxism of its powerful state support and let it exist of itself and stand on its own feet. And let all who wish to do so make propaganda for it, defend it, and din it into others without let or hindrance—but outside working hours and *not on state salaries*. In other words, the whole *agitprop* system of agitation and propaganda must cease to be paid for out of the nation's pocket. This should not anger or antagonize the numerous people who work in *agitprop:* this new statute would free them from all possible insulting accusations of self-interest and give them for the first time the opportunity to prove the true strength of their ideological convictions and sincerity. And they could only be overjoyed with their new twofold commitment: to undertake productive labor for their country, to produce something of practical value on weekdays in the daytime (and whatever work they chose in place of their present occupation would be much more productive, for the work they do now is useless, if not positively detrimental), and in the evenings, on free days, and during their holidays, to devote their leisure to propagating their beloved doctrine, reveling selflessly in the truth! After all, that is exactly what our believers do (while being persecuted for it too), and they consider it spiritually satisfying. What a marvelous opportunity, I will not say to test but to prove the sincerity of all those people who have been haranguing the rest of us for decades.

BUT HOW CAN ALL THIS BE MANAGED?

Having said all that, I have not forgotten for a moment that you are total realists—that was the starting point of this discussion. You are realists par excellence, and you will not allow power to slip out of your hands. That is why you will not willingly tolerate a two-party or multiparty parliamentary system in our country, you will not tolerate *real* elections, at which people might not vote you in. And on the basis of realism one must admit that this will be within your power for a long time to come.

A long time—but not forever.

Having proposed a dialogue on the basis of realism, I must confess too that from my experience of Russian history I have become an opponent of all revolutions and all armed convulsions, including future ones—both those you crave (*not* in our country) and those you fear (*in* our country). Intensive study has convinced me that bloody mass revolutions are always disastrous for the people in whose midst they occur. And in our present-day society I am by no means alone in that conviction. The sudden upheaval of any hastily carried-out change of the present leadership (the whole pyramid) might provoke only a new and destructive struggle and would certainly lead to only a very dubious gain in the quality of the leadership.

In such a situation what is there left for *us* to do? Console ourselves by saying "Sour grapes"? Argue in all sincerity that we are not adherents of that turbulent "democracy run riot" in which once every four years the politicians, and indeed the entire country, nearly kill themselves over an electoral campaign, trying to gratify the masses (and this is something which not only internal groups but also foreign governments have repeatedly played on); in which a judge, flouting his obligatory independence in order to pander to the passions of society, acquits a man who, during an exhausting war, steals and publishes Defense Department documents? While even in an established democracy we can see many instances when a fatal course of action is chosen as a result of emotionally inspired self-deception, or of a random majority caused by the swing of a small and unpopular party between two big ones—and it is this insignificant swing, which in no way expresses the will of the majority (and even the will of the majority is not immune to misdirection), which decides vitally important questions in national and sometimes even world politics. And there are very many instances today of groups of workers who have learned to grab as much as they can for themselves whenever their country is going through a crisis, and their country can go hang. And even the most respected democracies have turned out to be powerless against a handful of contemptible terrorists.

Yes, of course: freedom is moral. But only if it keeps within certain bounds, beyond which it degenerates into complacency and licentiousness.

And *order* is not immoral if it means a calm and stable system. But order too has its limits, beyond which it degenerates into arbitrariness and tyranny.

Here in Russia, for sheer lack of practice, democracy survived for only eight months—from February to October 1917. The émigré groups of Constitutional Democrats and Social Democrats pride themselves on it to this very day and say that outside forces brought about its collapse. But in reality that democracy was *their* disgrace; they invoked it and promised it so arrogantly, and then created merely a chaotic caricature of democracy, because first of all they turned out to be ill prepared for it themselves, and then Russia was worse prepared still. Over the last half century Russia's preparedness for democracy, for a multiparty parliamentary system, could only have diminished. I am inclined to think that its sudden reintroduction now would merely be a melancholy repetition of 1917.

Should we count as part of our democratic tradition the Land Assemblies in Muscovite Russia? Should we count Novgorod, the early Cossacks, the village commune? Or should we console ourselves with the thought that for a thousand years Russia lived with an authoritarian order—and at the beginning of the twentieth century both the physical and the spiritual health of her people were still intact?

However, in those days an important condition was fulfilled: that authoritarian order possessed a strong moral foundation, at least originally; it was not the ideology of universal violence, but Christian Orthodoxy, the ancient, seven-centuries-old Orthodoxy of Sergius of Radonezh and Nil Sorsky, before it was battered by Patriarch Nikon and bureaucratized by Peter the Great. From the end of the Muscovite period of Russian history and throughout the whole of the Petersburg period, once this moral principle was perverted and weakened, the authoritarian order, despite the apparent external successes of the state, gradually went into a decline and eventually perished.

But even the Russian intelligentsia, which for more than a century invested all its strength in the struggle with an authoritarian regime—what did it achieve for itself or for the common people by its enormous losses? The opposite of what it intended, of course. So should we not perhaps acknowledge that for Russia this path was either false or premature? That for the foreseeable future, perhaps, whether we like it or not, whether we intend it or not, Russia is nevertheless destined to have an authoritarian order? Perhaps this is all that she is ripe for today? . . . Everything depends upon *what sort* of authoritarian order lies in store for us in the future.

It is not authoritarianism itself that is intolerable, but the ideological lies that are daily foisted upon us. Not so much authoritarianism as arbitrariness and illegality, the sheer illegality of having a single overlord in each district, each province, and each sphere, often ignorant and brutal, whose will alone decides all things. An authoritarian order does not necessarily mean that laws are unnecessary or that they exist only on paper, or that they should not reflect the notions and will of the population. Nor does it mean that the legislative, executive, and judicial authorities are not independent, any of them, that they are in fact not authorities at all but utterly at the mercy of a telephone call from the only true, self-appointed authority. May I remind you that the *soviets,* which gave their name to our system and existed until July 6, 1918, were in no way dependent upon Ideology: Ideology or no Ideology, they always envisaged the widest possible *consultation* with all working people.

Would it be still within the bounds of realism or a lapse into daydreams if we were to propose that at least some of the real power of the *soviets* be restored? I do not know what can be said on the subject of our Constitution: from 1936 it has not been observed for a single day, and for that reason does not appear to be viable. But perhaps even the Constitution is not beyond all hope?

Still keeping within the limits of strict realism, I do not suggest that you alter the disposition of the leadership, which you find so convenient. But take all whom you regard as the active and desirable leadership and transform them *en bloc* into a *soviet* system. And from then onward let posts in the state service no longer depend on Party membership, as they do now. In doing so you can clear your Party of the accusation that people join it only to further their careers. Give some of your other hard-working fellow countrymen the chance to move up the rungs *without* having to have a Party card—you will get good workers, and only the disinterested will remain in the Party. You will, of course, want to keep your Party a strong organization of like-minded confederates and keep your special meetings conspiratorial and "closed" to the masses. But at least let your Party, once it has relinquished its Ideology, renounce its unattainable and irrelevant missions of world domination, and instead fulfill its national missions and save us from war with China and from technological disaster. These goals are both noble and attainable.

We must not be governed by considerations of political gigantism, nor concern ourselves with the fortunes of other hemispheres: this we must renounce forever, for that bubble is bound to burst—the other hemispheres and the warm oceans will in any case develop without us in their own way, and no one can control this development from Moscow or predict it even in 1973; much less can Marx do so from the perspective of 1848. The considerations which guide our country must be these: to encourage the *inner,* the moral, the healthy, development of the people; to liberate women from the forced labor of money earning—especially from the crowbar and the shovel; to improve schooling and children's upbringing; to save the soil and the waters and all of Russian nature; to reestablish healthy cities and settle the Northeast. Let us hear no more about outer space, no more historic victories of universal significance, and no more dreamed-up international missions: other nations are no more stupid than we are, and if China has money and divisions to spare—let her have a try.

Stalin taught us—you and all of us—that *affable complacency* was the "greatest of dangers," meaning that kind-hearted rulers were a very dangerous thing! He had to say that because it fitted in with his scheme of exterminating millions of his subjects. But if you have no such aim, then let us disavow his accursed commandment! Let it be an authoritarian order, but one founded not on an inexhaustible "class hatred" but on love of your fellow men—not of your immediate entourage but

137

sincere love for your whole people. And the very first mark that distinguishes this path is magnanimity and mercy shown to captives. Look back and contemplate the horror: from 1918 to 1954 and from 1958 to the present day *not one person* in our country has been released from imprisonment as a result of a humane impulse! If the odd one has occasionally been let out, it has been out of barefaced political calculation: either the man's spirit was completely broken or else the pressure of world opinion had become intolerable. Of course, we shall have to renounce, once and for all, the psychiatric violence and secret trials, and that brutal, immoral trap that the camp represents, where those who have erred and fallen by the wayside are still further maimed and destroyed.

So that the country and people do not suffocate, and so that they all have the chance to develop and enrich us with ideas, allow competition on an equal and honorable basis—not for power, but for truth—between all ideological and moral currents, in particular between *all religions:* there will be nobody to persecute them if their tormentor, Marxism, is deprived of its state privileges. But allow competition honestly, not the way you do now, not by gagging people quietly; allow it to religious youth organizations (*non*-political ones), grant them the right to instruct and educate children, and the right to free parish activity. (I myself see Christianity today as the only living spiritual force capable of undertaking the spiritual healing of Russia. But I request and propose no special privileges for it, simply that it should be treated fairly and not suppressed.) Allow us a free art and literature, the free publication of books (not of political books—God preserve us!—not exhortations or election leaflets); allow us philosophical, ethical, economic, and social studies, and you will see what a rich harvest it brings and how it bears fruit—for the good of Russia. Such an abundant and free flowering of inspiration will rapidly absolve us of the need to keep on belatedly translating new ideas from Western languages, as has been the case for the whole of the last fifty years —as you know.

What have you to fear? Is the idea really so terrible? Are you really so unsure of yourselves? You will still have absolute and impregnable power, a separate, strong, and exclusive Party, the army, the police force, industry, transportation, communications, mineral wealth, a monopoly of foreign trade, an officially set rate of exchange for the ruble—but let the people breathe, let them think and develop! If you belong to the people heart and soul, there can be nothing to hold you back!

After all, does the human heart not still feel the need to atone for the past? . . .

Perhaps it will seem to you that I have deviated from my initial platform of realism? But I shall remind you of my original assumption that you are not alien to your fathers, your grandfathers, and the expanses of Russia. I repeat: the wise heed advice long before the need becomes overwhelming.

You may dismiss the counsels of some lone individual, some writer, with laughter or indignation. But with each passing year—for different reasons, at different times, and in different guises—life itself will keep on thrusting exactly the same suggestion at you, exactly the same. Because this is a feasible and *smooth* way in which you can save our country and our people.

And yourselves into the bargain. For the hour of peril will come, and you will appeal to your people once more, not to world communism. And even your own fate—yes, even *yours!*—will depend on us.

Of course, decisions like these are not made

overnight. But now you still have the opportunity to make the transition calmly, over the next three years perhaps—or five, or even ten, allowing for the whole process. But that is only if you make a start now, only if you make up your minds this moment. For the demands life is going to make on you later will be even harsher and more pressing.

Your dearest wish is for our state structure and our ideological system never to change, to remain as they are for centuries. But history is not like that. Every system either finds a way to develop or else collapses.

It is impossible to run a country like Russia according to the passing needs of the day: in 1942 to condemn Nehru and his national liberation movement as a clique (for undermining the military efforts of our allies the English), and in 1956 to exchange kisses with him. And the same with Tito and with many, many others. To run a country like Russia you need to have a national policy and to feel constantly at your back all the eleven hundred years of its history, not just the last fifty-five—five percent.

You will have noticed, of course, that this letter pursues no personal aims. I have long since outgrown your shell anyway and my writings will be published irrespective of any sanction or prohibition by you. All I had to say is now said. I, too, am fifty-five, and I think I have amply demonstrated that I set no store by material wealth and am prepared to sacrifice my life. To you such a vision of life is a rarity—but here it is for you to behold.

In writing this letter I, too, am taking upon myself a heavy responsibility to Russian history. But not to take upon oneself the task of seeking a way out, not to undertake anything at all, is an even greater responsibility.

A. SOLZHENITSYN

5 September 1973

AN
INTERVIEW
WITH
ALEKSANDR
SOLZHENITSYN

BY JANIS SAPIETS

*Translated from the Russian
by Alexis Klimoff*

INTERVIEW WITH THE BBC, FEBRUARY 1979

On the fifth anniversary of Aleksandr Solzhenitsyn's departure from the U.S.S.R., the BBC Russian Service broadcast a conversation between
him and Janis Sapiets which took place at Solzhenitsyn's home in Vermont.

JANIS SAPIETS: *Aleksandr Isayevich, five years
have passed since your forcible deportation, not a
great amount of time from the perspective of history, but for a writer so closely tied to the fate of
Russia this is already a painfully long period. In
1967, at the meeting of the secretariat of the Writers' Union, you said, and I quote: "Throughout my
life I have had the soil of my homeland under my
feet; only* its *pain do I feel, only about* it *do I
write." Now that you are torn from this soil, could
one say, perhaps, that this pain has receded to the
past and has become more remote?*

ALEKSANDR SOLZHENITSYN: Everything has remained as if I had not been expelled. My life, my work, my orientation are the same as before.

In your book The Oak and the Calf *you speak about moments when you dreamed of going for years to some remote spot "amid fields, sky, forest, and horses, so as to write a novel unhurriedly." Has this dream come close to realization?*

Well, I suppose the "unhurried" part will never be realized in my life because I am behind schedule on the task I have set for myself, and I know that this task is a necessary one. Our entire generation is behind schedule in its task. As for the rest of the passage you quote, something of this sort has indeed been achieved. An externally peaceful life, no need for conspiracy, for hide-and-seek games, for the dispersal of papers; nothing but my work to be concerned about. Furthermore, all the historical materials which I had great trouble getting my hands on are now accessible.

It is said that you have completely withdrawn from reality, that you are leading an almost hermitlike existence. What has the West meant to you personally—freedom or new chains?

It's no easy matter to withdraw from contemporary reality; it scorches you on all sides. As you know, I have traveled widely and given speeches, but only because I've given in to temptation: I can't look on calmly as they surrender the whole world and themselves into the bargain. But ultimately that is not my concern, for there is much work to be done in our country. In terms of my project, yes, the West cannot supply me with any nourishing impressions. But if I could now live in Russia! and with the ability to move about freely, without being followed, without surveillance (as almost always used to be the case)—then of course I would lead a very different life than I do now: I would travel a great deal! In Russia every locality, every dialect, every meeting serves as an impetus and a help in my plan. But here there are only unnecessary distractions for which I don't have the years anymore. Fortunately in my time I walked the length and breadth of . . . What a situation: a city of three million but without a name! To say "Leningrad" seems shameful; I have no respect for the Emperor Peter either, but then again, the city was named for the apostle, not the emperor. . . . But there will be no return to the old Dutch appellation of "Sankt Pieterburkh" either.

. . . And to refer to it as "Piter," as people do today, is to repeat the name all the Bolsheviks used. I would call the city Nevgorod. That is in the spirit of the Russian language: Nevgorod, Novgorod. As I was saying, for two months I walked the length and breadth of the city, studying its historical places. The February Revolution took place almost completely in Petrograd, and today I can close my eyes and visualize any part of the city clearly; this helps a great deal. And of course I have an old map and many photographs.

Ten years ago, in a letter to Literaturnaya Gazeta, *you wrote that your one dream was to be worthy of the hopes placed upon you by Russian readers. What can Russian readers hope for from you now, when you have been abroad five years? What are you writing now, and what have the last few years brought you? What do you see as your work's meaning?*

My work began forty-three years ago, in 1936, when I had just left school. I had the idea then that I ought to describe and explain the October Revolution and the Civil War. Everything pointed to 1914 as the appropriate starting point, and I chose the Samsonov disaster. At the time, I thought I would soon get on to dealing with the October Revolution, although I did realize, even then, that there would have to be several volumes about 1917, since that was a year when every month was like a fresh epoch. But then many years got in the way of my writings: there was the war, prison, exile, illness, then all the persecution from the state, the struggle I was forced into waging, the other books I wrote about that period of my life. So *August 1914* grew into two volumes, *October 1916* into another two, and thus I fell more and more behind.

Only when I moved to America, three years ago, did I start seriously on the February revolution. And as soon as I got into it, everything appeared in a new light. I had been longing to get to the October Revolution, thinking February was just a stage on the road to it, but then I realized that the unfortunate experiences of February, the comprehension of what happened then—that is what our people need most of all at the present time.

We have failed to understand the February revolution, we have forgotten its lessons and not taken heed of them. There is a whole tangle of legends about this period. Indeed, the whole of our modern history has been presented to us in the form of fabrications and legends, not accidental ones, but deliberately made up. There is the legend that the Tsar was carrying on negotiations with the Germans for a separate peace—but there was never anything of the kind. Nicholas II, in fact, lost his throne because he was too loyal to England and France, too loyal to that senseless war of which Russia had not the slightest need; he allowed himself to be drawn into that atmosphere of militarist madness which reigned in liberal circles at the time. And these liberal circles were anxious to get their Western allies out of trouble at the expense of the lives of Russian peasants—they were afraid of getting a low rating from the Allies.

Then there is the legend that a soviet of workers' deputies was elected in February. The soviet, which had a thousand members, had no importance, for it was not able to undertake any practical decisions; everything was done by the small executive committee, to which the top people elected themselves. These second-rate, pitiful party-minded socialists elected themselves to power, and then led Russia into the abyss.

Then we come to the Provisional Government, legendary in the bad sense. These were the same liberal statesmen who, for years, went on protesting that they were worthy to represent Russia, that they were wonderfully clever, that they knew everything there was to know about how to guide Russia, and that, of course, they were far superior to the Tsarist ministers. In fact, they turned out to be a collection of spineless mediocrities, who let things slide rapidly into Bolshevism.

If you look into it, you find that it wasn't just that they let the power slip out of their hands—they were never able to seize the power in the first place. The Provisional Government actually existed, mathematically speaking, for minus two days; in other words, it completely lost control two days before it was set up. The whole February revolution was the work of the two capital cities; the entire peasant country, the entire active army, only learned with bewilderment about the revolution after it had happened. Furthermore, there never was a Kornilov revolt—that was just Kerensky's lies and hysterics; he made up the whole crisis. He himself summoned the troops from the front line to Petrograd, but then, because he was frightened of the left elements, he disclaimed responsibility for the troops when they were halfway to Petrograd and declared that a mutiny had taken place. And Kornilov never ran away; while Krymov trustingly came to see Kerensky, and met his own death. There was no mutiny, but thanks to his hysterics, Kerensky finally confirmed the Bolsheviks in power.

Yes, but surely, Aleksandr Isayevich, our whole conception of the history of Russia, at least in the West, is based on the assumption that the February revolution was a positive phenomenon, and that had it not been for the October coup d'état, Russia would have proceeded along the path of peaceful social development?

That is one of the central legends. If you go into the day-by-day story of events of February, into every detail, into the situation as it really was, then it immediately becomes clear to you that that revolution was going nowhere except into anarchy. There were contradictions in its every aspect. The amazing thing about 1917 is the story of how the February revolution collapsed of itself. The liberal-socialist rulers of Russia brought her to a state of complete collapse within six months. From the beginning of September 1917, the Bolsheviks could have seized power with their bare hands, without any difficulty. It was only because of the excessive caution shown by Lenin and Trotsky that they waited before doing so. The easy way in which they took power was not even a coup d'état. Therefore, not only was there no October *revolution;* there wasn't even a genuine coup. The February revolution fell unaided.

Yet the legend exists, and even has a continuation: the Civil War is quite incorrectly assumed to have been just a war between Reds and Whites, whereas, in reality, the most important thing was the popular opposition to the Reds in the years 1918 to 1922—a war in which, according to modern reckoning, 12 million people were lost. That amounts to a change in the composition of the people. And this was the first real, irrevocable revolution—when twelve million people were knocked out, selectively. But the legend tells us that it was the October Revolution which gave the peasants the land—whereas, in fact, it took away from them the land Stolypin had given them, as well as the community land.

Yes, but at the same time, surely all this is past history and, moreover, a narrow section of history which affects only Russia. And surely it is now the case that the majority of your readers are in the West. So who are you writing for?

I am very glad that a lot of people in the West read what I write. But my main readership is, of course, in my own country, and it is for them that I am writing. My books will reach them in time; indeed, quite a few have reached them already. Without any doubt, I shall soon return to my native land through my books and, I hope, in person too. As to the lessons of the February revolution, they are of worldwide significance; the West should find them useful too. The way in which our Russian liberals and socialists gave way to the Communists has been repeated on a worldwide scale since those days. The only difference is that the process has been spread out over several decades. The same process of self-weakening and capitulation is being repeated on a massive scale.

But for our country, the experience of February, and indeed of the whole of 1917, is truly paramount; and yet hardly anyone is thinking about it. Before we start hotly arguing about the future of Russia and suggesting schemes and recipes, we ought to know our own past really properly. But as a rule, Russians who argue about the future don't know their past, for the history of the present century in Russia has been concealed from us to such an extent that we are practically illiterate

—and we have accepted this situation. Under Soviet pressure, our historians have gone further back, to the era of Nicholas I and earlier, and anyone who has been officially studying the present century has been distorting everything. We ought to know about the February events and be warned by them: a repetition of February would be an irreparable catastrophe. It is important that everyone should understand this before any changes begin to take place in the state apparatus.

And thus it has turned out that my historical work on the February revolution—it takes up four volumes—was so very late that it has once again become relevant to the present.

You have been talking of the paramount importance of February; but how can an understanding of past experience really help us in our present situation?

Oh, such an understanding could be very important. The inward victory always comes first, before the outward one. We really don't have in Russia the physical strength at the moment to throw off the great weight which is crushing us. But the most valuable benefit of the last sixty years of world history has been the liberation from socialist

contagion which our people have experienced.
And our liberation from that contagion can be the
start of a worldwide process of liberation which
can affect even those countries that have not yet
contracted the disease.

Yes, we are still the prisoners of communism,
and yet for us in Russia, communism is a dead dog,
while for many people in the West, it is still a living
lion. We have in Russia withstood this period of
trial spiritually and, amazingly, we are still stand-
ing! Of course, it is not enough for us to fully understand communism: we are all still being stifled
by it, and we have to think about the dangers of
the transitional period which lies ahead of us. During that period, we are threatened with further
trials, for which we are completely unprepared.
These dangers will be of quite a new type for us,
and in order to withstand them, we should at least
have a proper knowledge of Russia's experience in
the past. It is possible that my voice at this moment is being heard by people who have the ac-
cess, the opportunity, and the time to study our
twentieth-century history. I am at present arrang-
ing the publication of a series of scholarly books
under the title *Studies in Modern Russian History*.
In this series, a number of authors, both old and

young, are trying to discover, purify, restore that truth which has been stolen from us, suppressed and distorted. I hope that writers will be found inside the U.S.S.R. also who would like to take part in this series. I am convinced that all the most important conclusions about our history are destined to be born inside Russia, despite the terrible restrictions prevailing there. If anyone hearing my voice now is or will be engaged in work of this kind, the address is: Russian Memoir Library, P.O. Box 1446, Boston, Massachusetts 02101.

That bears on the historical legacy. But what is your opinion about the present situation in Russia with regard to literature?

During these last few years, while I have been in exile in the West, I have been impressed and delighted by the Russian literary writings that have been coming out. And this successful writing has been achieved not by the free émigré writers, not through the abundance of so-called self-expression, but back in our Russian homeland, where writers are aching under enormous pressure. Moreover, this success has been achieved in what is the real heart and core of Russian literature—in that area which Soviet literary critics half con-

temptuously refer to as the "literature of the countryside." This is, in fact, the most difficult area
attempted in the works of our Russian classic writers. It is in this area that there has been some
outstanding Soviet writing in the last few years,
despite all the restrictions. I could easily name five
or six of these writers and give the titles of their
books (some of them have written more than one)
and an analysis of their achievements. But speaking as I am from America, I have no right to do
that in a broadcast to Russia; the authorities would
start reproaching those writers: "It's not for nothing that Solzhenitsyn is praising you," and so on.
But I think the authors concerned, and their readers too, will understand of whom I am speaking.

It can be hard for us to appraise the standard of
contemporary literary writings. But such a level in
the depiction of peasant life from the inside, how
the peasant feels toward the earth around him,
toward nature, toward his own labor—such a level
of unforced, organic imagery, springing straight
from the life of the people—such a level of poetic,
rich, popular language—this was the level to
which our Russian classic writers aspired, but
which they never achieved, not Turgenev, nor
Nekrasov, nor even Tolstoy. Because they them-

selves were not peasants. For the first time, peasants are writing about themselves. And now readers can enjoy the finest pages of these authors.

Here is an interesting anecdote. There is, here in America, an association of Slavists who study our country, and they hold annual conferences at which many new émigrés hasten to make speeches. One of these émigrés is Klepikova, who declared with an authoritative tone at a conference, in reply to a question about the "literature of the countryside": "Literature of the countryside? Oh, nowadays that has declined into decadence, into imitation of old forms." And the American professors who had come to this conference from all over the country trustingly wrote down in their notebooks: "The literature of the countryside is in decline." And this at a time when, in fact, it is flourishing! That is how some of the new émigrés talk about our country; that is the use they are making of their freedom to speak out.

Perhaps my words will be heard by those young writers who are destined in the future to move our literature forward. I would like to say to them: There is no need to strive after superficial political satire—that is the very lowest form of literature. There is no need to look for new forms; avantgardism does not, in fact, exist—it has been thought up by empty-headed people. What you need to do is to develop a feeling for your own native language, for your native soil, your native history—all this will provide more than enough material, and the material itself will dictate the form the writer should use.

Another sad anecdote. In the autumn of 1977, during the American book exhibition in Moscow, some American publishers decided to give an official dinner for the most eminent representatives of Russian literature. But the guest list was drawn up on this principle: who is reckoned to be a dissident? And so, ironically, no representatives of the real core of Russian literature were invited. Of those writers whom I just listed in my mind, not one was asked—they are not even known. The idea was to give a dinner in honor of Russian literature; but there were no leading Russian authors present. I could add the names of at least two first-class playwrights who are active today in the Soviet Union; but again, I don't want to harm them by naming them.

But is this "real core of Russian literature," as you have called it, understood in the West?

Not very well. The official agency representing Soviet literature abroad does not represent it at all. Or else there is impenetrable stupidity: they send some literary jailer who had abused Tvardovsky as a "kulak poet" even in the last year of his life, but who now claims to worship his memory. And American professors take notes on the nonsense this jailer tells them.

There also exists an overdeveloped resourcefulness in maneuvering between the Soviet regime and the intellectual West, an ability to be appreciated by both. I have in mind Voznesensky, for example, who cheerfully allows himself to be exhibited and thus helps create the impression of literary freedom in the U.S.S.R.

I once told Voznesensky that he had no Russian soul. He simply lacks one. His heart is tormented neither by the past misfortunes of Russia nor by the present ones. He had a poem about the slaughter in the Guyanese commune published in the U.S.A. It's bad enough that he depicts them in angelic colors, but it is positively insulting that in this corrupt fanaticism and degeneration he claims to have glimpsed the self-immolation of the Russian Old Believers. . . . What can one say to that? The Old Believers perished in order to remain true to their faith and so they would not be driven by torture to accept another. But no one was touching these Marxists, no one was trying to drive them anywhere, and their entire conflict with the U.S. was imaginary. In this way he belittled the Old Believers in order to be fashionable, because American newspapermen had been making such comparisons. A wooden heart, a wooden ear.

In your Harvard commencement address you contrast the weakening of human personality in the West with its growing strength in the East, where, and I quote, "the complex and deadly crush of life has produced stronger, deeper, and more interesting personalities than those generated by standardized Western well-being." But has not this "deadly crush of life" also caused spiritual devastation, has it not brought about cynicism and materialism, has it not maimed thousands and even millions of personalities? How can one then speak of a spiritual renaissance in Russia? Is this idea not a dream? Might it not reflect a wish rather than reality?

Yes, of course, no one could have lived through communism without injury. We have all experienced this and millions have been spiritually harmed. (But I would add a qualification here: harmed, yes, but not in the infectious socialist sense. No voice is strong enough to summon us in that direction anymore: our minds and hearts have been exposed to *that* din long enough to cause nausea.)

What did I mean at Harvard about character and personality? How would we define a strong personality? Here is my opinion: It is strong if in the most hostile of circumstances and almost without help from the outside it can endure and have enough strength left over to offer it to the outside. And the absence of character? This would involve receiving everything in the most favorable circumstances and keeping it all for oneself. In Berlin in 1953 and in Hungary in 1956 there were Russian officers and men who refused to turn their weapons against the people, although they knew that they would be shot for it, and so they were. A monument to their memory stood for a while in West Berlin, but the feckless West gave in here too, and removed the stone in the interests of détente.

When I spoke about our greater strength of character compared with that of the West, I had in mind that we have learned beneath the dragon itself, we don't bend; while they bend at a distance from its breath alone, the better to placate it.

Yes, we have been injured, many of us *almost* irretrievably so. And yet *not* irrevocably! This is shown by the revival of our society. Right now I have in mind not the intellectual and political animation, not samizdat, not the various letters of protest, but the change of atmosphere around those who are persecuted. For fifty years those who were sentenced or doomed were completely cut off from society: not only could one not help, but one even avoided communicating with them. Communism depended on the individual perishing by himself. And today? Every such family today receives offers of help from all sides, money is collected, there is open assistance and visits without attempts at concealment. And this is a completely different moral atmosphere; we seem almost not to be living under the Soviet regime. These shoots are even coming up in the provinces, where things are in general much more sinister, and where the wind howls more ominously. The younger generation has been much affected by this process of purification; therein lies the hope for the future.

I would say that such changes are more profound and have greater long-term significance than a revolution. People are behaving as if these vampires and the dragon above them no longer existed. A new atmosphere!

———◆———

Aleksandr Isayevich, as you know, an émigré is often full of bitterness. He has lost the ground from under his feet and lives only in the past.

Ivan Ivanovich, I am not an émigré. I took no such spiritual decision as to leave my homeland and start a new life somewhere else; so I have a different outlook.

Yes, but I am talking about emigration in general. It is a social phenomenon with its own—as it believes—historical mission.

The first wave of emigration did, of course, have a historical mission: to help us preserve a historical memory of the prerevolutionary and revolutionary years at a time when everything in the Soviet Union was being trampled underfoot. But as for the third wave of emigration, for example, I doubt that it does have a historical mission.

The third wave of emigration is merely the tail end, the splinter, of the emigration to Israel. In significance and numbers, it bears no comparison with the first two waves. Anyway, the salvation of Russia can stem from no group of émigrés—nothing will come of that! It will come from within Russia itself.

I hope that next time, in contrast to 1917, the country's fate will be decided by those who live there and not by those who return from emigration. Not everybody understands that voluntary departure greatly diminishes that person's right to judge and influence the fate of the country he has left. If he leaves, he has cut himself off. If he divests himself of responsibility, he also divests himself of his right. But the country continues to work out its own fate.

I have always said that the third wave of émigrés left not to escape the bullet (like the fighters of the first wave) and not to escape the noose (like those of the second); they left at the very time when opportunities for action emerged in our country and when forces were most needed there. The

Communist regime cannot be overcome from outside, only from within.

Among those who left there were, of course, various categories. The vast majority of people simply left to lead a better life; they were indifferent to the country they were leaving. A very small but politically active part seems to continue in the West action for the democratic human rights movement, but they find themselves in a situation where they are asking their neighbors to give them help back home. Heavens, what can the West do to help us? What can it do—they should be saving themselves!

The activities of this group of émigrés, living in freedom, are marked by a lack of vision. You cannot reduce all your philosophy and all your activities to: "Give us rights!" In other words: "Free our tied hands!" Suppose they did, or we tore loose—what then? Here the democratic movement shows its ignorance of modern Russian history. In effect, it overlooks all the lessons of our history as though they had never been. Following the general theory of liberalism, they simply want to repeat the February revolution—and that means ruin.

Then there is the category of those who left with a fierce hatred, not of the Soviet system, but of Russia itself, of its very people. They even cursed the country as they left, like the so-called Telegin —a pseudonym; his identity is known. Over here they vent their hatred in print; the word "orthodoxy" sends them into convulsions. But I don't want to talk about these overt activists.

There is, however, one dangerous category which perhaps is fulfilling a historical mission. They come here not just as émigrés but as fullfledged interpreters and explainers of our country, our people, history, culture, and so on. A typical characteristic is that they very soon sense the fashion and what people want from them. At the same time, their conclusions are always extremely useful for the Communist regime in the U.S.S.R.

But can't we assume that they, to some extent, still express their own sincere views and offer their own answers to the crucial issues of Russia's fate?

I will not guess at the real motivations of this category of émigrés. But just consider: those who cooperated with the Nazis are put on trial, but those who, for decades, cooperated with the Communists, who were all steeped in their Little Red

Book—these people are welcomed in the West as the best of friends and experts, although the academic level of many of them is that of the barbershop. With some variations, their general line is this: to do everything they can to reconcile the Americans with communism in the U.S.S.R., on the grounds that it is, for Americans, the least evil and even a positive phenomenon. On the other hand, they try to convince people that a Russian national renaissance, even the national existence of the Russian people, is the greatest danger for the West.

There is a whole string of people like this—too numerous to name. For instance, take Yanov. For seventeen years, he was an obscure Communist journalist. But here in America, he became a university professor. He has already published two books analyzing the U.S.S.R. and is extremely hostile to everything Russian. The *Washington Post* devoted a whole column to his article declaring that Brezhnev is a peace-lover. The message of his books is: Hang on to Brezhnev with all your might, support the Communist regime by trade and diplomacy and strengthen it, for it is advantageous to you Americans. Inside the U.S.S.R., the regime is supported by all those who buy at the "Beryozka" shops, and any other regime in Russia will be the worse for you.

Yanov does not even reproach the Communist regime for annihilating sixty million people. He has picked up the little word "Gulag," but he applies it to old Russia—there was a Gulag for you, he says. All his arguments proceed from the basis of goods and consumption. In his books, for instance, you will find no hint that the Russian people might have some sort of religion or that this might have some significance in its history and its aspirations. And these are the lips that interpret Russia over here! These are the flowers that communism has raised from our oblivion and degradation.

Yet intellectual America lionizes them because people here expect and want it to be like that: they want to make friends with communism and believe that Russia is bad. One after the other, American professors repeat: "At last, erudite scholars have come and explained to us what we must fear—not communism at all, but the national existence of the Russian people." In such an atmosphere over here it is impossible, for example, to mount an international defense of Igor Ogurtsov.

*But American—no, not just American, but West-
ern educated society in general—at least, part of
it—is informed of the true situation. How do you
explain the fact that they yield so easily to such
influences?*

American educated society tends to listen to such
persuasion, first because there is a long tradition of
speaking ill of national Russia. From the end of the
last century this tradition was created by Milyukov
and then by all revolutionary émigrés. It reached
such a pitch that in the First World War, American
banks granted loans to Britain and France with
the proviso that these credits would not find their
way to Russia, their ally.

Secondly, there is the American intellectuals'
great sympathy for socialism and communism.
They almost all live and breathe it. To be a Marxist
in an American university today is an honor, and
there are many university departments that are
Marxist through and through.

Thirdly, such an interpretation comforts the entire West. If all the horrors in the U.S.S.R. stem,
not from communism, but from the unfortunate
Russian tradition, from Ivan the Terrible and
Peter, then the West has nothing to fear. It follows

that nothing bad will happen. If socialism does overtake them, then only a virtuous socialism!

Since the unmasking of the Soviet system, Western concepts have retreated from trench to trench. First they abandoned Stalin and shifted all the blame onto a mythical Stalinism which never existed. Then, with a heavy heart, they abandoned even Lenin: if everything bad stemmed from Lenin, it was not, they argue, because he was a Communist, but because he was Russian. Since these are all Russian perversions, what has the West to fear? The West is very afraid of hearing the truth—any truth. The West is much given to reassuring self-deception.

Then, the intellectual West's sympathy for the Soviet system is also conditioned by the common source of their ideological origins: materialism and atheism. A movement openly connected with religion always alarms, if it does not scare them. This attitude on the part of the American academic world also bars them from understanding the essence of Russian history, although they argue about it with assurance as though they had already thoroughly grasped it, as though one could understand it while ignoring ten centuries of Orthodoxy. Western liberty would seem to give them advantages beyond compare with lying, dense Soviet scholarship, and yet they seem to be hypnotized by the Soviet conception of history. Involuntarily, they adopt its fundamental tenets and use them as arguments to correct particulars, details, aspects, personalities, and, sometimes, interpretation.

But if some field is completely banned in the U.S.S.R., as though it were nonexistent, it also remains quite unknown to Western scholarship. For example, for fifty-five years, brilliant Western scholarship knew nothing about the Gulag, had no conception of its scale, did not believe that it existed. For example, the Bolsheviks declared the popular resistance to their rule "banditry," and Western scholarship adopted the term "scattered banditry." It even overlooks completely the extensive popular resistance to the Bolsheviks.

Here is a shattering case in point: One young American scholar, in recent years, wanted to defend a thesis on "Popular resistance to the Bolsheviks and the civil war in Siberia." Everyone turned him down and at last they explained why: "No university would ever accept such a suspect thesis." The boy gave in and asked: "Well, give me a topic, then!" And they did: "The Party education network in the U.S.S.R." Back home, any chicken;

the meanest turkey—let alone a child—would laugh at such a topic. But in an American university, this is a thesis!

It would probably be fair to say that the lack of Western understanding of the situation in the Soviet Union has led to the conflict which has marked your meeting with the West. Three years ago, you warned the West, and Britain in particular, of the possibility—or rather the inevitability—of a moral and spiritual collapse under the thrust of totalitarianism. The same idea of the West's spiritual bankruptcy was echoed in your Harvard speech last year. Does this mean that your experience of life in the West—in Europe and America—has confirmed your view that the West is doomed?

No, not doomed, but by and large, the scales are tilted to the bad. We are clearly moving toward a world war, yet Western statesmen deceive themselves that we are moving toward détente. They surrender several countries a year to communism, and yet they do not tremble. What is this? How long will the supply of countries last? Can forces emerge in the West to awaken and restore it to health? I still hope so. If not, I would not be issuing warnings.

I particularly hope for the United States, where there are many untapped, unawakened forces quite unlike those which operate on the surface of newspaper, intellectual, and metropolitan life. For example, the people reacted to my Harvard speech in quite the opposite way to the way the newspapers did. There was a great flood of letters to me and the editors in which the readers mocked their newspapers' attitude.

But taking the West as a whole, don't you see some glimmers of enlightenment, particularly among young people, in religious circles?

Yes, I agree. In various places, in various phenomena, here and there you do notice that Western young people are more sensitive to the truth than their teachers, for all their diplomas. These young people seem to be able to forge through the welter of rubbish, striving and seeking. In many of them, religion arouses not a smile, but interest, sympathy, even involvement. And of course, we must consider the new Pope a banner of the time. It's . . . words fail me . . . it's a gift from God!

But things have been so neglected, the West's withdrawal has gone so far, that it is fruitless for us, in our country at any rate, to count on Western assistance. I thought this when I was still in the U.S.S.R. and had never appealed to either Western leaders or Western parliaments. I cherished no such illusions. In individual cases, assistance can come from public opinion, but nobody in the West is obliged to concern himself with us as a whole problem. Nobody has either the strength or the fortitude. And if they feel the need to trade us off, they will do so—as with Taiwan.

If this is so, where is the source of strength for prisoners seeking freedom? To whom or to what should they turn? What can they rely on? What can the peoples under Soviet rule hope for?

That is the hardest question you have put to me. On the one hand, I feel that we have already won the main victory over communism—we have stood out for sixty years and not been infected by it. There has been nothing like that ideological triumph, that massive conquest of souls, that Lenin and Trotsky talked of and counted on. Already, we are mentally free of them. But physically . . . Changes in our country are difficult precisely because the entire life of mankind turns on our country. When changes occur in the Soviet regime, the whole orbit of life on earth will change. We are now the nodal point of all human history.

In The Oak and the Calf, *you also ask whether the time has not at last come when Russia will begin to awake—when Birnam Wood will move. Has Birnam Wood moved?*

Again, this depends on how you regard movement. Spiritually—yes, it has moved; physically—no, it has not. But I have never advocated physical general revolution. That would entail such destruction of our people's life as would not merit the victory obtained.

We must do more than free ourselves; we must embark on the path of healing—and revolutions do not heal. Moreover, the ordinary citizen in our country is in a position where he cannot be urged to join physical movements; they would threaten his very life. That is why I urged the movement to *Live not by lies.* Cease supporting their ideology so that it crumbles and collapses. This will also be tantamount to changing the regime. The movement is developing, and God grant that it may continue to do so, but it has proved slower than I expected. By its very nature, it cannot be a rapid movement.

In your "Letter to the Soviet Leaders," you spoke of the possibility of free competition between Communist and other ideologies. How do you regard this after your five years' experience in the West?

You know, speaking of my "Letter to the Soviet Leaders," it is time I gave some explanation. To answer your specific question: that was really an ironic passage. No ideological competition with communism can emerge in our country because, ideologically, communism has already lost everything. In my "Letter to the Soviet Leaders," it was a joke that, in their free time after real work—and without pay, of course—the Party propagandists would propagate communism. I was simply joking. They are so concerned with Number One that —without payment—they wouldn't lift a finger, even for their own ideology. The main element in the "Letter to the Soviet Leaders" was not spelled out but implied: that I was actually appealing not to those leaders. I was trying to map out a path which could be taken by other leaders—not the current ones—who might suddenly come to replace them. This whole issue cannot be considered in general, divorced from the present world situation.

In what tribulations will these selfish leaders yet involve us! The Communists cannot renounce aggression. It is in progress now: the devilish growth of armaments—guns which begin to fire themselves.

These madmen may well succeed in plunging both our country and the whole world into war. They are doomed to repeat the mistake of all conquerors throughout world history: they imagine they are so strong that they can seize the whole known world, but each time they are wrong. They will be wrong this time too. In actual fact, they will destroy the whole world, ruin our people and still suffer defeat. But how? Because ranged on the opposite side will be a billion-strong China. Hence, the victor will again be communism, but in a different form.

The Americans are nurturing China into a world conqueror, just as they nurtured Soviet communism after the Second World War, to rebound on their own heads. So salvation brooks no delay. Every further year of their rule wreaks irreparable harm: now they have ruined the Baikal; next they plan to ruin Siberia by reversing the Siberian rivers. They are exhausting the country, misdirecting the people's efforts, each year clouding and spoiling millions of young souls. For every Communist year that passes we shall have to pay with several years of recuperation. We, too, must not delay.

What do you yourself rely on, Aleksandr Isayevich? What do you believe in? In Providence?

I would not take the name of Providence in vain. When you pronounce that word, you enter a solemn sphere. I am convinced of His presence in every human life—in my own and in that of entire peoples. But we are so superficial that we can understand nothing in time. We discern and understand all the zigzags of our life very, very belatedly. I am convinced that, someday, we will also understand the purpose of 1917.

In our country, I count on that degree of enlightenment which has already developed in our people and must inevitably extend also to the spheres of the military and the administration. A people, after all, is not just a throng of millions down below, but also its individual representatives occupying key posts. There are sons of Russia up there too, and Russia expects that they will fulfill their filial duty. This stratum of society must realize that any war of aggression will be our national downfall.

I well recall our officer corps in the Second World War: how many ardent, honest hearts completed that war with the urge finally to build a better life in our homeland. I cannot believe that they have all vanished without trace, like water into the sand, and that they or their heirs are indifferent to the dreadful fate that is being prepared for our country—the disastrous international venture into which it is being driven.

I believe in our people at all levels—wherever they may be. It cannot be that the 1,100-year existence of our people will not, in some as yet unknown form, overcome the sixty-five-year frenzied sway of the Communists. Our strain is the stronger, and we must overcome them and shake them off. This might even occur at the height of a future war; but a thousand times better if forces can be found within the country to stop aggression before it even starts.

And how do you see Russia's future?

I see it in *recuperation*. Renounce all mad fantasies of foreign conquest and begin the peaceful, long, long, long period of *recuperation*.